50 YEARS
lonely planet
OF TRAVEL

POCKET

MARRAKESH

TOP EXPERIENCES • LOCAL LIFE

T0043503

HELEN RANGER

Contents

Plan Your Trip   4

Moroccan architecture on show
LIFESTYLE TRAVEL PHOTO/SHUTTERSTOCK ©

Explore Marrakesh 35

Survival Guide 143

Special Features

Welcome to Marrakesh

Prepare to be dazzled by the city that has it all. From the razzamatazz of Djemaa El Fna to museums grand and small, glorious riads, entrancing souqs, tranquil gardens, a vibrant food scene and a dash of new city glamour – once you have succumbed to the charms of the Red City, it's hard to let go.

Souq near Djemaa El Fna (p38)

Top Experiences

Join the carnival at Djemaa El Fna (p38)

Gawp at the superb Ben Youssef Medersa (p82)

Wander through Jardin Majorelle (p120)

DEL BOY/SHUTTERSTOCK ©

SAIKO3P/SHUTTERSTOCK ©

Take in the grandeur of Bahia Palace (p94)

Discover old Marrakesh at Maison de la Photographie (p84)

CHRIS GRIFFITHS/LONELY PLANET ©

MAURIZIO DE MATTEI/SHUTTERSTOCK ©

Marvel at Koutoubia Mosque (p42)

Swat up on carpets at Dar Si Said (p44)

MICHAEL BIGGS/GETTY IMAGES ©

Appreciate design at Musée Yves Saint Laurent (p124)

musée YVES SAINT LAURENT marrakech

Explore the Saadian Tombs (p96)

FALEPHOTOGRAPHY/SHUTTERSTOCK ©

JON CHICA/SHUTTERSTOCK ©

Dining Out

Marrakesh's culinary scene is one of the country's most exciting and diverse. That said, since traditionally Marrakshis don't eat out often, most medina restaurants are aimed squarely at the tourist market, and meals can be hit-and-miss. In middle-class Gueliz, there's more of a local dining vibe with both Moroccan and international restaurants.

Street Food

Streetside snacking is a way of life in Marrakesh, so don't be afraid to jump in. Busy souq workers with no time for a long lazy lunch head to a *snak* (street stall; pictured) to feast on peppery *merguez* (spicy sausage), *teyhan* (stuffed spleen) and *brochettes* (kebabs). Hot spots in the medina (besides Djemaa El Fna) include just south of Place Ben Youssef in the souqs, Rue de la Kasbah and the western end of Rue Bab Doukkala.

Riad Dadas

The *dadas* (cooks) who work in the medina's riads are the unsung heroes of Marrakesh's culinary scene. Many riads open up their courtyard or rooftop restaurant to nonguests so you can sample different cooks' takes on Moroccan specialities. In nearly all cases, you have to book ahead because of both limited seating and so the *dada* can plan the menu in advance.

Best Cheap Eats

Zeitoun Cafe Always buzzing for its delicious food, overlooking Djemaa El Fna. (p51)

Marrakech Henna Art Cafe Good-value sandwiches and Berber omelettes. (p52)

Chez Kamal & Brahim A local grill stand that moonlights as a tourist restaurant. (p103)

Best Vegan & Vegetarian

La Famille Three-course menu of the freshest souq produce served under the lemon trees. (p50)

Mandala Society Innovative, organic Moroccan/Icelandic menu and fair-trade coffee. (p50)

World Storytelling Café Listen to stories over tapas, soups and vegetable dishes. (p41)

CURIOSO/SHUTTERSTOCK ©

Best Global Eats

+61 Freshest ingredients in inventive dishes served in light-filled, airy surroundings. (p135)

I Limoni Excellent pasta dishes served up in this citrus-tree-shaded courtyard. (p114)

Vita Nova Good Italian dishes including homemade pasta, with a glass of wine. (p135)

Best Modern Moroccan

L'Mida Delightful riff on local cuisine. (p89)

Terrasse des Épices Great twists on Moroccan favourites on a sunny rooftop. (p71)

Le Jardin Greenery and birdsong add to the delicious menu of classics and new ideas. (p70)

Best Riad Dining

La Table Al Badia Dinner menus concocted from what's available in the medina souqs. (p105)

Pepe Nero Charming service and courtyard dining beside the pool with both classic Italian and Moroccan menus. (p50)

La Table du Palais Candle-lit meals under a canopy of palms. (p73)

Best Local Faves

Amal Center Cooking with a cause – one of Marrakesh's top lunch spots. (p134)

Naima Superior couscous made fresh daily. (p89)

Mechoui Alley Slow-roasted lamb straight from the pit oven. (p52)

Dining-Out Details 🍴

○ Alcohol is becoming more accepted in medina restaurants, but most still don't serve it.

○ Book ahead for top-end restaurants and trendy spots, particularly in peak season (March to May and October to December).

Treasure Hunt

Marrakesh is one of the world's great shopping destinations. The full gamut of Moroccan crafts – both traditional and contemporary – can be found here, and few travellers return from a trip empty-handed. In the souqs, haggling is the name of the game, but some medina boutiques and all the Gueliz design shops have fixed prices.

Souq 101

'Souq' means 'market', but when locals refer to 'the souqs', they mean the maze of market streets north of Djemaa El Fna and southwest of Musée de Marrakech. Prices are at their most expensive in Souq Semmarine (Leather Souq), the main thoroughfare from Djemaa El Fna, because of the high price of real estate (and tourist traffic) on the main drag. Products here often come from specialist souqs just a few streets away.

It is always better to buy in dedicated souqs, especially carpets, metalware and leatherwork. The smaller *qissariat* (covered markets) between Souq Smata and Souq Nejarine usually have lower-priced crafts. The streets south of Djemaa El Fna, Riads Zitoun El Kedim and Jedid can be more pleasant places to shop, but the choice isn't quite as broad.

Best for Modern Design

Souq Cherifia Young designers pitch their claim on the upper balcony selling quirky accessories and homeware. (p76)

Different. The medina goes hipster at this fun fashion and accessories boutique. (p75)

Wafl Design Tongue-in-cheek prints, t-shirts and homewares with sassy slogans. (p57)

Best for Beauty

Aromatimri Organic essential oils, argan and prickly pear oils and face and body treatments. (p57)

Naturom Heavenly potions and lotions, all fully organic and locally made. (p56)

L'Art du Bain Savonnerie Artisanale Luxurious soapy stuff with Moroccan scents. (p76)

HEMIS/ALAMY STOCK PHOTO ©

Best Co-op Shopping

Assouss Cooperative d'Argane Gorgeous argan oils to slather over skin, sold by a women's cooperative. (p78)

Al Nour Delicately embroidered cotton clothing, stitched by artisans with disabilities. (p75)

Best for Carpets

Bibi Art Three-storey carpet emporium that employs its own Atlas Mountain weavers. (p77)

Soufiane Zarib Towers of carpets in a cavernous showroom, with production overseen and quality controlled by the designer. (p78)

Best for Fashion

Sissi Morocco Unique silky-soft tees featuring sepia photos of Amazigh (Berber) tribal women. (pictured; p74)

Norya Ayron Floaty caftans in bold prints and silky fabrics so you can always feel you're in Morocco. (p79)

Les Marrisiennes Playful prints use Moroccan icons such as *babouches* (leather slippers) and fez hats. (p56)

33 Rue Majorelle The best selection of local designers in the city, no question. (p140)

Worth a Trip

If you dream of kitting out your house like a Marrakesh riad, head 4km out of the central city to the industrial district of **Sidi Ghanem** (p140). Here the streets are crammed with local designer factory outlets and showrooms selling modern spins on Moroccan ceramics, textiles and beauty products, as well as traditional crafts. Negotiate a taxi rate of Dh300 to Dh350 for the round trip from the medina, and pick up a map of the quarter at an open showroom.

Art & Design

Marrakesh is a city steeped in ancient artistry. Palaces are a riot of mosaics, painted wood and carved decoration; riads display intricate plasterwork and textiles. These craft traditions are kept alive by the modern artisans of the souqs and also inspire the contemporary art and design scene, well established in Gueliz and now storming through the medina.

Traditional Techniques

Tour any historic monument in Marrakesh and its opulent interiors are guaranteed to inspire artistic reverence. The palaces are a riot of *zellige* (colourful geometric mosaic tilework), *muqarnas* (decorative plaster vaulting) and *zouak* (painted wood). Also look out for *tadelakt,* a satiny, hand-polished limestone plaster used in riads that is now employed in contemporary ceramics.

Contemporary Art

Trailblazing Marrakesh is the centre of Morocco's small but growing modern-art scene. Marrakesh's contemporary artists merge abstract with tribal art forms and Arabic calligraphy and motifs. Gueliz has become a hive of independent art galleries, and the **1-54** (Contemporary African Art Fair; 1-54.com), held at La Mamounia in February, attracts around 6000 visitors a year.

Best for Artists at Work

Ensemble Artisanal Head here for a gander at local craftspeople and artisans at work. (pictured; p141)

Souq Haddadine The medina's blacksmiths have their workshops here. (p77)

Best Galleries

Comptoir des Mines Galerie Gueliz' biggest and best contemporary art gallery is inside this three-floor, art deco building. (p132)

Musée de la Palmeraie Large collection of modern Moroccan sketches, paintings and sculpture in lovely gardens. (p133)

Musée Farid Belkahia Well-curated selection of works from one of Morocco's most

HOLGER LEUE/GETTY IMAGES ©

lauded 20th-century artists. (p133)

Maison de la Photographie A glorious photographic journey through Moroccan landscapes and community heritage. (p84)

Dar Bellarj Old stork hospital converted into a nonprofit community art centre. (p89)

MACMA Traces the history and artistic vibrations of Morocco through photography and the decorative arts. (p132)

Best Artisan Interiors

Bahia Palace It ain't called 'The Beautiful' for nothing, you know. (p94)

Saadian Tombs An interior that was worth dying for. (p96)

Musée de la Musique A jewel-box of domestic interior design restored to its Saadian-era glory. (p69)

Ben Youssef Medersa Centuries-old school with courtyard surrounded by swirling stucco, carved wood and *zellige*. (p82)

Art & Craft Workshops

If you've fallen hard for Morocco's artisan crafts, consider booking a short workshop through **Ateliers d'Ailleurs** (ateliersdailleurs. com) to try making your own. The company works with a handpicked network of professional artisans in crafts such as pottery, *tadelakt*, woodwork, *zellige*, brassware and more. You'll get a unique insight into traditional techniques and the opportunity to chat with the artisan one-on-one (with a translator). Workshops are private and hands-on, running for either three or five hours.

Spas & Hammams

The quintessential Moroccan experience: after a day of dusty sightseeing exploits, try this centuries-old Moroccan ritual involving a steam bath, wash and vigorous gommage (scrub-down) that leaves you squeaky clean, fresh and invigorated. Join locals at the public hammam if you're feeling adventurous, or treat yourself at a private spa-style hammam.

Hammam History

Public baths were first introduced to Morocco and the rest of North Africa by the Romans. After Islam gained a foothold across the region, the baths were adapted to fit in with Islamic ablution rituals – foregoing the communal Roman bathing pool to use running water to wash under instead.

In past centuries, hammams were the only source of hot water in the medina. Traditionally they are built of mudbrick, lined with *tadelakt* (satiny hand-polished limestone plaster that traps moisture) and capped with a dome that has star-shaped vents to let steam escape. They are usually adjacent to the neighbourhood mosque and community oven: all three often share the same water and heating infrastructure.

Public or Private?

For many Moroccans public hammams are as much a social occasion (particularly for women) as they are about bathing.

They cost around Dh10 to enter, are always single-sex and are in constant use, day in, day out, so not always in the best state of repair. Some tourists baulk at the experience, which can feel like taking a bath (nude or semi-nude) with the entire neighbourhood. Yet they're usually clean and no other experience in Marrakesh will get you behind the veil of local life quite like the public hammam. Private hammams, on the other hand, are essentially Moroccan-flavoured spas. A traditional hammam

CHRISTIAN GOUPI/ALAMY STOCK PHOTO ©

experience, conducted in private, at one of these venues costs from about Dh350. Both public and private hammams also offer optional massages.

Best Public Hammams

Hammam Mouassine The best choice for public hammam newbies, with charming staff used to travellers and bath-and-scrub packages. (p66)

Hammam Bab Doukkala Historic public hammam dating from the 17th century: a truly local experience. (p113)

Best Private Hammams

La Sultana Spa Opulent marble-clad interiors and numerous pampering treatments and massage packages. (p102)

Hammam de la Rose Friendly staff, relaxed ambience and a host of add-on beauty and massage options. (pictured; p70)

Le Bain Bleu Stylish surroundings and luxurious spa-like services. Go on, treat yourself. (p69)

Heritage Spa A bevy of rejuvenating deep-cleansing treatments are on offer at this swish spa. (p113)

Hammam Tips

o Public hammams are usually open for women during the day and men during the evening, though there are some exceptions to the rule.

o It's best to book ahead for private hammams. Many private hammams offer package deals for couples.

o For more tips, see p68.

Courses & Tours

The breadth of tours on offer in Marrakesh is hard to beat: you can chow down on street food with a local, learn Arabic calligraphy or explore city backstreets on two wheels. Marrakesh's close proximity to mountains, palm groves and sands also makes it an excellent jumping off point for active adventures such as trekking and mountain-biking.

LEILA MELHADO/GETTY IMAGES ©

Best for Food

Atelier Chef Tarik (atelier-chef-tarik.com;) A farm-to-table rural culinary school a half-hour drive from Marrakesh, with relaxed kilim-cushion garden seating, a bucolic organic farm and cooking tent. The price includes transfers.

Marrakech Food Tours (marrakechfoodtours.com) Local hosts take groups of up to six participants on a whirlwind tour of Marrakshi flavours via medina walking tours, or let them whisk you to an Atlas Mountains village for a local meal.

Faim d'Epices (https://faimdepices.com) A fun day on a countryside farm just outside Marrakesh, learning about spices (and how to tell if your saffron is the real thing), before cooking a three-course meal and breads. Transport is provided.

Clock Kitchen (Cafe Clock; cafeclock.com) Shop in the souq for ingredients, then it's back to Cafe Clock for a fun morning cooking up a storm. Eat a slap-up lunch of your efforts around 2pm. A bread-baking and patisserie workshop is also available.

Best Cycling Tours

AXS (argansports.com;) Classic city rides through the Palmeraie, cycling tasting tours, and mountain biking in the Atlas Mountains (as well as trekking options), plus bike hire. High-quality Giant road bikes, mountain bikes (including kids' bikes) and helmets are provided.

Marrakech Bike Action (marrakechbikeaction.com) Organises tour circuits of the city and Palmeraie, as well as mountain-biking day trips and longer excursions. The company also has electric-assisted mountain bikes.

Pikala Bikes (Map p110, D2; pikalabikes.com) Rent a bike for your own exploration, or join a 2½-hour tour through the medina streets. It also has tandems, mountain bikes, and group bikes

RAW-FILMS/SHUTTERSTOCK ©

that come with a guide. Bike tours into the High Atlas are available.

Best Outdoor Excursions

Inside Morocco Travel (insidemoroccotravel. com) Bespoke adventures designed by multilingual Mohamed Nour and his team, specialising in trekking trips into the High Atlas and combined 4WD excursions exploring the desert and mountains. Can cater for families.

Tawada Trekking (tawadatrekking.com) Multiday trekking tours into the Atlas Mountains, rafting trips and cultural immersion experiences are the speciality of this small, professional company run by Hafida H'Doubane, one of the first Moroccan women to be licensed as a mountain guide.

Insiders Experience (insidersexperience.com) Hop in a vintage motorbike sidecar on these off-the-beaten-track tours of the city, desert and Atlas Mountains, or combine a ride with a hot-air balloon excursion (pictured).

Mountain Voyage (mountain-voyage.com) This British-owned company organises tailor-made Marrakesh tours and High Atlas excursions with stays at its own property, the Kasbah du Toubkal.

Responsible Travel

Moroccans are rightly proud of their heritage and visitors support and amplify this. However, it's better not to support practices such as the snake charmers and exploitation of monkeys on Djemaa El Fna. Being aware of the effects of overtourism and buying from local organisations are some of the ways in which you can travel responsibly.

MATTES RENÉ/HEMIS.FR/ALAMY STOCK PHOTO ©

Overtourism

Bottlenecks of tour groups at Marrakesh's top sights are often poorly managed and put stress on the city's historical heirlooms. Make an effort to stray off the tourist path and visit some of Marrakesh's excellent, often overlooked, smaller museums and attractions.

Consider an early morning visit to the Jardin Majorelle (p120) to beat the crowds: it opens at 8am. It's now essential to buy a ticket online for the garden and the neighbouring Yves Saint Laurent Museum (p124) which saves queuing at the entrance.

Stay longer and venture beyond the city for waterfall walks, mountain trails and village meals. You'll put money into the pockets of rural communities, experience fewer crowds and see a completely different side to Morocco.

Support Local and Give Back

Stay in small riads in the medina which employ local people and buy local goods and services. Consider donating to international organisations that work locally, such as the High Atlas Foundation (high atlasfoundation.org), which is involved with sustainable development, or Education For All (efamorocco. org), which helps girls in rural communities go to school.

Buy from women's cooperatives that employ vulnerable women, those with disabilities and women from rural areas with few work opportunities. You can buy direct from the women artisans at The Anou

ANDREW NASH/WIKI COMMONS ©

(theanou.com) or take part in one of their workshops. Take a cooking class at **Amal Targa** (pictured right; http://amalnonprofit.org). a non-profit organisation which supports vulnerable women and trains them in restaurant skills.

Take the kids to the **Jarjee Donkey Refuge** (jarjeer.org), just outside Marrakesh, to see the irresistible baby donkeys.

Avoid quad biking as it has a devasting effect on the flora and fauna in the Palmeraie and on beaches and sand dunes elsewhere in Morocco.

Best Responsible Choices

Marrakech Food Tours Take a tour with this organisation supporting local families and industries. (p20)

Amal Center Have lunch at the Amal Center in Gueliz. (p134)

Assouss Cooperative d'Argane Visit this women's organic-certified argan cooperative. (p78)

Al Nour A women's cooperative run by local women with

disabilities offering textiles and homewares. (p75)

Cafe Clock Enjoy a concert here to support local musicians and community projects. (pictured left; p103)

Pikala Bikes Hire a bike from this outlet training young people to become professional cycling tour guides and bike mechanics. (p111)

World Storytelling Café Eat here to help save the precarious art of storytelling. (p41)

Pedal Power

Marrakesh's bike-sharing scheme, Medina Bike (p147), has more than a dozen bike stations all over the city and inexpensive passes for a day or a week.

Amazigh Culture

Marrakesh has Amazigh (Berber) roots, founded by the tribes of the Atlas Mountains who became the Almoravid dynasty. Through its long history this city has kept up its Amazigh connection, functioning over the centuries as a vital commercial hub where tribes came to buy and sell.

ILPO MUSTO/ALAMY STOCK PHOTO ©

Folk Music

To experience a slice of Amazigh culture while you're in Marrakesh, catch a folk music performance. Amazigh music uses a minimum of accompanying instruments, usually depending on a drum to set the rhythm and a flute to carry the tune. Because of the huge diversity of different tribes, there is a rich breadth of musical styles under the Amazigh umbrella.

The **National Festival of Popular Arts**, in July, is a great time to be in the city if you want to catch a variety of folk music groups. At other times, head to Djemaa El Fna (p38) in the evening. On any given night, the square plays host to some Amazigh musicians.

Best for Amazigh Culture

Jardin Majorelle Don't miss the stunning collection of Amazigh art, artefacts, jewellery and textiles at the Pierre Bergé Museum of Berber Arts inside Jardin Majorelle. (p120)

Musée Tiskiwin The vast scope of Amazigh art and culture is unveiled in this riad's displays. (pictured; p48)

Cafe Clock Every Saturday night from 6pm, this cafe in the Kasbah area hosts Amazigh bands. (p103)

Heritage Museum Amazigh textiles and artefacts make up part of the displays in this charming museum. (p49)

Dar Si Said The city's most comprehensive guide to carpet styles and motifs from the tribes of Morocco's mountains. (p44)

Djemaa El Fna Between the soothsayers and snake charmers, you'll find Amazigh musicians entertaining the evening crowds. (p38)

Bar Open

CHRIS GRIFFITHS/LONELY PLANET ©

Marrakesh doesn't have a huge nightlife scene, but in recent years, a few trendy bars have opened in Gueliz. The medina has only a handful of restaurants and bars licensed to serve alcohol, but many riads sell beer and wine to guests in the privacy of their inner courtyards. Sipping mint tea is the main nightlife drinking action for locals.

Best Medina Bars

El Fenn The best part about this super-stylish riad complex is the rooftop cocktail bar. (p73)

Kosybar Chill out with a beer while watching the storks preen themselves. (p105)

Café Arabe Head here for cocktails as the sun sets over the medina. (p74)

Le Foundouk Hidden in the central medina, this restaurant inside a restored *funduq* (inn once used by caravans) has a dedicated bar area. (p89)

Kabana Rooftop bar with views of Koutoubia Mosque, local flavour and lively beats. (p53)

Best Gueliz Nightspots

68 Bar à Vin You don't have to be a vino expert to enjoy this fun wine bar. (p138)

Barometre Marrakech Descend the stairs to this subterranean bar that thrives on experimental cocktails. (p137)

MY Kechmara Check out Marrakesh's youthful, arty crowd at this hip rooftop hangout. (pictured; p138)

Nightlife Need-to-Know

o Marrakesh clubs are eye-wateringly expensive, many are outside the main city area (meaning pricey to get to by taxi), and most don't kick off until after midnight. Our advice is don't come here to club.

o Most venues serving alcohol expect guests to eat as well as drink, especially those in the medina.

o Morocco has a surprisingly large wine and brewing industry. The local wines and beers are easy to find and worth a try.

Country Getaways

MALEO PHOTOGRAPHY/SHUTTERSTOCK ©

The daily grind of Marrakesh can be challenging for visitors, so if you're staying a few days consider a poolside jaunt out in the country. Day packages at retreats around the city can be the perfect antidote to souq hassle and medina dust. These palm-fringed bolt-holes can also offer a mellow alternative to staying in the medina.

Beldi Country Club (pictured; beldicountryclub. com; 👤) Popular eco-chic paradise with pools (including one for kids), spa, hammam, curated souq shopping and a restaurant (serving alcohol). It's 6km south of central Marrakesh; transfers cost Dh100 each way from the medina.

Ferme Berbère (https:// lafermeberbere.ellohaweb. com/; 👤) Loll on a sun lounger at this rustic adobe-walled retreat with lunch sourced from its gardens. It's a great option for families: lunch for two adults and two children, pool access, family hammam and donkey rides for the kids cost Dh910 (transport extra).

Riad Bledna (riadbledna. com; P 🏊) The garden villa of the Moroccan-British

Nour family is a low-key country retreat that also offers superb-value day packages (per person including lunch and transfer €30). The rate includes delicious home cooking with garden produce, and use of the big oxygen-filtered pool.

Casa Taos (casataos.net; P 🎵 🏊) Hicham and his foodie family ladle out lashings of hospitality at this colourful villa with beautiful rooms. Day guests (Dh200 per person, or Dh385 with à la carte lunch; book ahead)

can submerge themselves in the large pool under swaying palm trees. Transfers are about Dh100 one way (up to three people).

Jnane Tamsna (jnane. com; 🎵 🏊) Sustainability meets jet-setting style at Meryanne Loum-Martin's nine-acre country pad, with numerous swimming pools and tennis courts set in landscaped gardens. Three-course organic lunch with pool access for Dh495/295 per adult/child.

What's Included?

○ Day packages will include towels, a poolside sun lounger and use of shower facilities.

○ Most options include lunch but not drinks; book at least a day ahead.

For Kids

The mutual admiration between kids and Marrakesh is obvious. From the palm-studded riad gardens and their tinkling fountains to fairy-tale souq scenes and the spectacle of Djemaa El Fna, wonderment is everywhere. Much of the medina can only be explored on foot, so bring a backpack for babies and toddlers.

MICHAEL HEFFERNAN/LONELY PLANET ©

Medina Outings

Take the kids on palace jaunts, splash in the garden fountains, and pause for freshly squeezed juices on cafe rooftops to take in the lilting call to prayer. From 6pm to 8pm is the best time for Djemaa El Fna dance troupes and musicians (pictured), and the possibility of chance encounters with Moroccan families.

Best for Kids

Creative Interactions (creative-interactions.com) Join a task-filled medina hunt, family henna-art workshops, or Moroccan Arabic classes.

Oasiria (oasiria.com) Beat the heat at this water park with eight pools, a kamikaze slide and a pirate lagoon.

Atelier Chef Tarik (atelier-chef-tarik.com) Kids will love the organic kitchen gardens and farm animals at this rural cooking school.

Terres d'Amanar (terresdamanar.com) This outdoor centre offers zip lines, mountain biking and horse riding.

Family Travel Tips

o Pushchairs are impractical in the medina, baby-changing facilities nonexistent and few restaurants have kids menus. Speeding motorbikes can be dangerous for toddlers.

o Book private hire cars through your accommodation to guarantee seatbelts for locking in car seats.

o Riads are not childproof, but many cater to families, and staff dote on little ones.

o Early mornings are quieter in the souqs, meaning less hassle and a better view of craftspeople at work.

Four Perfect Days

Day 1

CHRIS GRIFFITHS/GETTY IMAGES ©

Hit the central souqs in the morning when they're quiet. Sniff out spices at **Place Rahba Kedima** (pictured; p63), peek inside the *fanadiq* (inns once used by caravans) of **Dar El Bacha** (p67) and visit the palace museum before retreating to the Islamic gardens of **Le Jardin Secret** (p66).

In the afternoon, head south to the kasbah to view the glorious ceilings of **Bahia Palace** (p94). Climb the ramparts of the **Badi Palace** (p101) ruins, then visit the **Lazama Synagogue** (p101). Save the **Saadian Tombs** (p96) for when it is bathed in late-afternoon sunshine.

After dinner on **Djemaa El Fna** (p38), do a loop around the floodlit **Koutoubia Mosque** (p42) before returning for music on the square.

Day 2

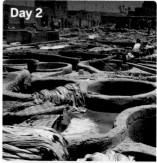

BOJAN KVEDER/LONELY PLANET ©

Get a taxi to Bab Debbagh and follow your nose to the acrid **tanneries** (pictured; p88). Afterwards, view a slice of old Marrakesh in **Maison de la Photographie** (p84) and the **Orientalist Museum** (p87). Visit the magnificent **Ben Youssef Medersa** (p82) and the adjacent **Musée de Marrakech** (p87).

Admire the restored finery on show at **Musée de la Musique** (p69) then trawl for souvenirs amid the cool boutiques of **Souq Cherifia** (p76) and in the vast concept store of **Different.** (p75).

Scrub off the souq dust and rejuvenate with a spa session at **Le Bain Bleu** (p69) or, if you're feeling brave, in the public **Hammam Mouassine** (p66).

Day 3

Make a dash for the bamboo groves and Pierre Bergé Museum of Berber Arts at **Jardin Majorelle** (pictured; p120) as early as you can manage but note you must book online at least 24 hours ahead. Get a combined ticket to visit the excellent **Musée Yves Saint Laurent** (p124) next door.

Spend the afternoon hunting out Gueliz' art deco architecture and contemporary-art galleries. Or head back to the medina to swat up on carpets at **Dar Si Said** (p44), and visit nearby **Musée Tiskiwin** (p48) for ethnographic exhibits from across North Africa.

Take a stroll through lively **Place des Ferblantiers** (p99) en route to **Cafe Clock** (p103) in the Kasbah district, to check out the evening's live music.

Day 4

Discover a quieter side of the medina amid the *derbs* (alleyways) that spiral off Rue Bab Doukkala before dropping into **Henna Cafe** (p114) to learn about Islamic henna art, and perhaps get some of your own. Or get active on a morning cycling tour through the medina with **Pikala Bikes** (p147).

Touring complete, do as the Marrakshis do to beat the heat and head out of the centre for swimming and sunbathing amid the palm-shaded haven of the **Beldi Country Club** (pictured; p26): the perfect antidote for souq-weary feet.

Finish your Marrakesh adventure with an evening of medina rooftop drinking at swanky **El Fenn** (p74), lively **Kabana** (p53) or popular **Café Arabe** (p74).

Need to Know

For detailed information, see Survival Guide (p143)

Currency
Moroccan dirham (Dh)

Languages
Moroccan Arabic (Darija), Tamazight, French

Visas
Most nationalities do not require a visa for stays of up to 90 days.

Money
ATMs are widely available. Credit cards are usually accepted at top-end accommodation and restaurants, but not always in midrange riads. Expect to pay cash in shops except at top-end outlets.

Mobile Phones
Data coverage in Marrakesh is reliable.

Time
GMT/UTC plus one hour

Tipping
Tipping is an integral part of Moroccan life; almost any service can warrant a small tip of a few dirham.

Daily Budget

Budget: Less than Dh750
Budget double room: Dh300–450
Cheap museum entrance fees: Dh30–50
Tajine at a canteen: Dh50–75
Evening entertainment at Djemaa El Fna: free, plus tips

Midrange: Dh750–1400
Riad double room: Dh550–900
Three-course set-lunch menu: Dh120–170
Glass of wine: Dh60–90
Half-day cycling tour: Dh350

Top end: More than Dh1400
Double room in a boutique riad: from Dh1800
Dinner in palace-style restaurant: Dh550–800
Cocktail at a bar: Dh150–200
Private hammam soak and scrub: from Dh250

Advance Planning

Three months before Book riad accommodation; particularly important if travelling in high season (October to December, March to May). Most riads have only four to six rooms.

One month before Organise activities such as cooking classes (most have limited space); book tickets online for Jardin Majorelle and Musée Yves Saint Laurent.

One day before Check the weather. Marrakesh gets colder than you think in winter, and fiercely hot in summer.

Arriving in Marrakesh

✈ Marrakesh Menara Airport

Airport bus 19 (Dh30) runs to Djemaa El Fna every 30 minutes between 6.15am and 9.30pm. *Petits taxis* wait outside the arrivals hall but drivers often charge inflated rates; consider booking a transfer through your accommodation.

🚃 Marrakesh Train Station

The metered rate for a taxi is about Dh15 from the station (pictured) to the medina, but taking a taxi waiting at a stand will cost more. Establish the price before you get in. City bus 10 (Dh4) runs to Djemaa El Fna every 20 minutes or so between 6am and 10pm.

🚌 CTM & Supratours Bus Stations

Taxis wait inside the bus car parks. Most will quote Dh50 to Djemaa El Fna. You can catch city bus 10 from Ave Hassan II to Djemaa El Fna.

Getting Around

🚶 Walk

Marrakesh is flat, and the central area is small, making it easy for walking. Most of the medina is a car-free zone.

🚗 Taxi

Creamy-beige *petits taxis* are abundant and the quickest way to travel. Drivers usually use the meters, but are not required to from a taxi stand; so hail one on the street. If you do take one at a taxi stand, negotiate the cost before you get in.

🚃 Bus

Cheap and frequent but hot and overcrowded; useful for hops between Gueliz and the medina.

Calèche

Horse-drawn carriage rides are a scenic option for trips between Djemaa El Fna and sites such as Jardin Majorelle.

Marrakesh Neighbourhoods

Musée Yves Saint Laurent 👁

Jardin Majorelle 👁

Gueliz & Ville Nouvelle (p119)
Modern Marrakesh offers art galleries, top restaurants and shady parks to escape the hurly-burly of the medina.

Bab Doukkala & Riad Laârous (p107)
With its daily produce market and alleyways filled with street art, Bab Doukkala is Marrakesh's friendliest and most interesting residential neighbourhood.

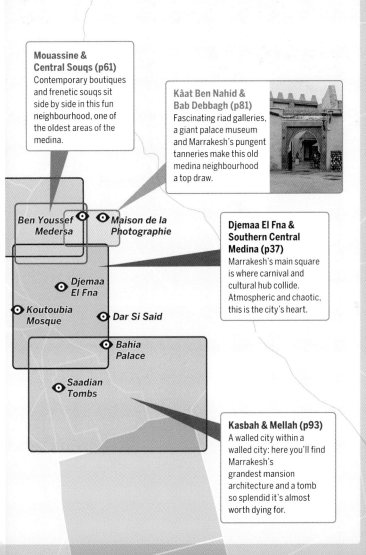

Mouassine & Central Souqs (p61)
Contemporary boutiques and frenetic souqs sit side by side in this fun neighbourhood, one of the oldest areas of the medina.

Kâat Ben Nahid & Bab Debbagh (p81)
Fascinating riad galleries, a giant palace museum and Marrakesh's pungent tanneries make this old medina neighbourhood a top draw.

Ben Youssef Medersa

Maison de la Photographie

Djemaa El Fna & Southern Central Medina (p37)
Marrakesh's main square is where carnival and cultural hub collide. Atmospheric and chaotic, this is the city's heart.

Djemaa El Fna

Koutoubia Mosque

Dar Si Said

Bahia Palace

Saadian Tombs

Kasbah & Mellah (p93)
A walled city within a walled city: here you'll find Marrakesh's grandest mansion architecture and a tomb so splendid it's almost worth dying for.

Explore
Marrakesh

Marrakesh's Walking Tours 🥾

Marrakesh's Cycling Tour 🚲

A traveller exploring Marrakesh OSCAR WONG/GETTY IMAGES ©

Djemaa El Fna & Southern Central Medina

Roll up, roll up: if there's one thing you can't miss in Marrakesh it's the reeling, free-wheeling circus that is Djemaa El Fna. At night, hordes of hungry revellers come to chow down at food stalls. Heading south, the parallel Riad Zitoun roads and surrounding alleyways are crammed with interesting shops.

The Short List

○ **Djemaa El Fna (p38)** *Diving into the thronging crowds after dark to experience the fizzing energy of the square.*

○ **Koutoubia Mosque (p42)** *Staring up at the architectural beauty of the Koutoubia minaret.*

○ **Dar Si Said (p44)** *Learning the weaves and wefts of Moroccan carpets at this revamped textile museum.*

○ **Mechoui Alley (p52)** *Joining the throngs of local lunchers clamouring for slow-cooked lamb.*

○ **Musée du Patrimoine Immatériel (p48)** *Finding out more about the performers on Djemaa El Fna.*

Getting There & Around

🚶 Djemaa El Fna is roughly in the centre of the medina and most streets lead here.

🚗 Taxis can drop off directly in the main square until midday.

🚌 The most direct routes to Djemaa El Fna are via No 1 (from Gueliz) and No 11 (from Bab Doukkala).

Neighbourhood Map on p46

Top Experience 📷

Join the Carnival at Djemaa El Fna

Welcome to the greatest show on earth. Everywhere you look in Marrakesh's main square, you'll discover drama in progress. It's been this way for almost a millennium: a hypnotic dance of hoopla, halqa (street theatre) and food stalls, set to the tune of gnaoua drums and snake charmers with their piercing flutes.

◉ MAP P46, D3110

History

Djemaa El Fna sprang into life in the 11th century, around the time that the city of Marrakesh was founded by the Almoravids. Historians and locals will argue over whether the square got its name from the fact that public executions were likely held here: one translation is 'assembly of the dead'. Another translation is 'mosque of the dead', which could be a nod to the partial collapse of neighbouring Koutoubia Mosque in the 18th century (p43), burying worshippers inside.

For centuries, the square was used as a giant food market, with traders flooding down from the mountains to set up under canvas tents each day. Early photos of this era can be seen in Maison de la Photographie (p84). The present boundaries of the square were imposed by the French, as all the buildings surrounding the Djemaa were erected during the protectorate era.

Morning Quiet

Stroll Djemaa as it wakes up to catch the plaza at its least frenetic. At this point, the stage is almost empty. Fruit-juice vendors are first on the scene, along with the snake charmers and their baskets of cobras. Incense and potion sellers and henna-tattoo artists start setting up makeshift stalls under sunshades.

Night-Time Carnival

Local food stalls start setting up for the nightly dinner scrum around 4pm. At sunset, the Djemaa finds its daily mojo as Amazigh troupes and gnaoua musicians start tuning up and locals pour into the square. The hullabaloo doesn't knock off for the night until around 1am. To view it from a different perspective, head to one of the rooftop cafes ringing the square.

★ Top Tips

o Keep a stock of Dh10 coins on hand to tip performers. A few dirhams (a little more if you take photos) is all that's necessary.

o Arrive early in the evening to nab prime seats on makeshift stools (women and elders get preference).

o Stay alert to motorbikes, cars and horse-drawn-carriage traffic before 2pm, as well as pickpockets and rogue gropers.

o Be warned that you will see chained monkeys paraded for tourists, and the practices of the snake charmers are ethically questionable.

✕ Take a Break

o If you feel your energy flagging, head to the terrace of Grand Balcon du Café Glacier (p54) for a mint tea.

o For serious munching, follow your nose to Chez Lahmine Hadj Mustapha (p52) for the best *tanjia* in town.

Cultural Collapse on Djemaa?

Djemaa El Fna has been a protected urban landmark since 1922 and Unesco-inscribed since 2001 as a place of unique cultural exchange. Yet Unesco has flagged the square as a space under 'serious threat' from urbanisation and cultural assimilation.

For centuries, Djemaa has been a stage for gnaoua dance troupes, whispering fortune tellers, cartwheeling acrobats and, above all, *hikayat* (storytellers). Today, the last of the storytellers have gone and with them many of the square's traditional performers. Djemaa is still the throbbing heart of the medina, but like its inhabitants, it's moved with the times. Live music and local food are its 21st-century trademarks. Learn more about the history of these performers at the Musée du Patrimoine Immatériel (p48) on the edge of the square.

Dinner at Djemaa

Spicy snail broth, skewered hearts, bubbling tajines, flash-fried fish: the Djemaa food stalls are a heaving one-stop shop for Moroccan culinary specialities, and they're not to be missed. Despite alarmist warnings, your stomach should be fine as hygiene requirements are scrupulously upheld. Clean your hands before eating, use bread instead of utensils and stick to filtered water.

Stalls have numbered spots and are set up on a grid. The snail chefs are in a line on the eastern side. For fried fish and calamari, pull up a pew at stall 14. Look for a lovely lady called Aicha who runs stall 1

Moroccan culinary speciality – snails

Saving Djemaa's Storytellers

Marrakesh has a strong tradition of *hikayat* (oral storytelling). For centuries, history soaked in myth, as well as fictional ancient epics of heroic derring-do and morality tales, have been passed down through the generations by storytellers whose narrative skills were highly prized and sought after. This popular art form was not just for entertainment. It was a vital tool for passing on knowledge about the wider world.

Djemaa El Fna is thought to have been firmly established as a central platform for storytellers by the 11th century. It is because of this age-old tradition that Unesco declared Djemaa El Fna a 'Masterpiece of World Heritage' in 2001.

But today there are no storytellers left on the square. In the 20th century, the advent of radio, television and the internet eroded their once-important role. Djemaa El Fna's traditional storytellers, who spent years learning their craft, are retired or have died. The city's famed square is now a hub for more boisterous performances and musical acts.

A resurgent interest in saving *hikayat* from extinction has recently emerged. A project at Cafe Clock (p103) has partnered Djemaa storytellers with a group of young local apprentices who perform the tales in English, bringing the rich art of Moroccan storytelling to a wider audience. It's an electrifying evening and well worth your time. The **World Storytelling Café** (https://worldstorytellingcafe.com; 🔗) also hosts storytelling sessions, and organises the Marrakech International Storytelling Festival.

boilerplate: MUPART/SHUTTERSTOCK ©

in the southwestern corner for *brochettes* (kebabs), tajines and *harira* (a cheap, hearty soup made of tomatoes, onions, saffron and coriander with lentils, chickpeas and lamb).

After dinner, join locals at the row of copper tea urns on the southern edge of the stalls. The speciality here is warming ginger tea called *khoudenjal* with cinnamon, mace and cardamom, served with a dense, sticky and similarly spicy scoop of cake – a pit stop at No 71 Chez Mohammed's is the perfect way to round out your meal.

Shopping South of Djemaa

Running in parallel, south from the Djemaa El Fna, Rues Riad Zitoun El Jedid and Riad Zitoun El Kedim are both excellent places to shop. You can get most of the same artisan wares on these streets as in the northern souqs, but the sellers are more laid-back, and there are fewer tour groups here. Recently Riad Zitoun El Kedim has also acquired a cluster of upmarket, fixed-price shops selling contemporary Moroccan homewares, clothes and beauty products.

Top Experience 📷
Marvel at Koutoubia Mosque

Five times a day, the voice of the Koutoubia's muezzin rises above the Djemaa din, calling the faithful to prayer. The Koutoubia Mosque's minaret has been standing guard over the old city since the Almohads erected it in the 12th century. Today it's Marrakesh's most famous landmark. Gaze up in awe at the ornate decoration by the minaret's Almohad-era builders.

◉ MAP P46, A5

Minaret: An Ancient Design Icon

This 75m-high tower has quite the reputation as an architectural muse. It's the prototype for Seville's Giralda and Rabat's Le Tour Hassan. Unlike Middle Eastern mosques, which have domed minarets, the Koutoubia's square design is an Amazigh trademark. Crane your neck to check out its scalloped keystone arches and jagged merlon crenellations.

There are no stairs inside the minaret, only a ramp that the muezzin would have once ridden up on horseback to give the call to prayer.

The Spire

The minaret is topped by a spire of brass balls filled with special mineral salt from the High Atlas Mountains, which includes nitrate and magnesium that prevents the spire from oxidising. The salt is changed once a year, during Ramadan, to maintain the golden glint. In front of the spire, the wooden stick points toward Mecca (all mosques in the medina have this feature) and is also used to bear flags on religious holidays.

Prayer Hall Ruins

On the northwestern side of the minaret are the ruins of the mosque's original prayer hall. One story goes that it collapsed during the massive 1755 Lisbon earthquake, killing hundreds of people as it crumbled. Scientific research also suggests this is plausible. To the north of the Koutoubia minaret, the original doorway still stands. On the far wall of the ruins the remains of the arches that would have held up the ceiling are visible. The stumps on the floor are the hall's columns, and they stay in situ as a memorial.

In Arabic, *djemaa* means congregation as well as gathering, and one theory is that the true translation of Djemaa El Fna is not 'assembly of the dead', but 'mosque of the dead', a legacy of the tragic event that occurred here.

★ **Top Tips**

○ Non-Muslims can't enter the mosque or minaret, but you're most likely to get a glimpse inside if you come on a Friday when the doors are flung open for prayers.

○ The best spot from which to photograph Koutoubia's minaret – framed by old stone and date palms – is under the archway to the left of the main entrance.

○ If you're feeling frazzled by all the Djemaa El Fna action, the palm-studded Koutoubia Gardens (p49) directly behind the mosque are a soothing respite.

✕ **Take a Break**

○ Refuel with a sugar fix at Pâtisserie des Princes (p52), lauded for its pastries (though its ice cream is delicious too).

○ For a refreshing mint tea with a view of the minaret, head across the road to lovely old-fashioned Café El Koutoubia (p53).

Top Experience 📷

Swat Up on Carpets at Dar Si Said

This 19th-century medina mansion was once home to Si Said, brother to Vizier Bou Ahmed of Bahia Palace (p94) fame. Although artistically similar, Dar Si Said is much more intimate than its sibling site. The mansion is now home to Morocco's well curated National Museum of Weaving and Carpets, so it's essentially two attractions for the price of one.

◉ MAP P46, F5

fnm.ma

Ground Floor Galleries

Make your first stop the wall map that pinpoints the different carpet-producing regions of Morocco. The plain ground-floor galleries are divided into regions: High Atlas for high-quality wool, natural colours and decorative motifs inspired by the environment; Middle Atlas for geometric designs using black, white, blue and green; Anti Atlas for multicoloured band rugs and woollen carpets.

Floor-to-ceiling textile displays also cover Marrakesh Haouz, Oriental carpets from the far north and rural weaving rich with Amazigh symbols. Informative displays, explaining symbolism and weaving techniques, are supplemented by film projections. There's also a large area for temporary exhibitions in the western wing.

Inner Courtyard

The ground-floor galleries lead out into a peaceful inner courtyard, where a central fountain sits under a wooden gazebo with an intricately painted ceiling. Bordering the courtyard, ornately decorated arched doorways lead into rooms holding collections of Berber jewellery, 19th-century armaments and rural weavings.

Wedding Chamber

Climb the narrow staircase to the 1st floor to visit the spectacular painted and domed wedding reception chamber, credited to artisans from Fez. Here musicians' balconies flank the vast main salon boasting exuberantly coloured cedar-wood ceilings. The upper floors of the mansion display urban carpets and a full-scale wooden loom. Nearly identical looms can still be found in some traditional workshops, such as Fibre Trip (p91).

★ Top Tips

o If you ran into tour group crowds at Bahia Palace and are regretting not spending more time admiring the painted cedar-wood ceilings and ornate plaster-work artistry, don't fret. Dar Si Said's upstairs rooms are home to excellent examples of *zouak* (painted wood) work, and the elaborate arched doorways of the central courtyard are worthy artistic contenders.

o Plan to visit Musée Tiskiwin (p48) at the same time; it's only a two-minute walk away.

✗ Take a Break

o Scoot back towards Djemaa El Fna down Rue Riad Zitoun El Jedid for a sandwich and beer at Un Déjeuner à Marrakech (p53).

o Alternatively, sample authentic Lebanese dishes at Naranj (p50).

Djemaa El Fna & Southern Central Medina

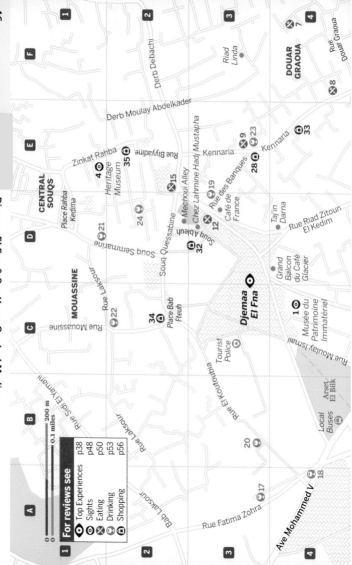

For reviews see
Top Experiences   p38
Sights   p48
Eating   p50
Drinking   p53
Shopping   p56

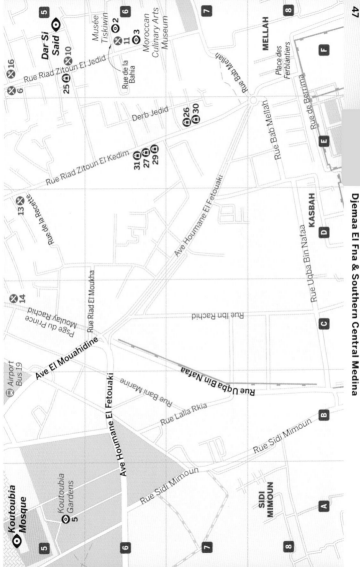

Djemaa El Fna & Southern Central Medina

Koutoubia Mosque

Koutoubia Gardens
5

Rue Sidi Mimoun

SIDI MIMOUN

Rue Sidi Mimoun

Rue Lalla Rkia

Rue Bani Marine

Ave Houmane El Fetouaki

Ave El Mouahidine

Airport Bus 19

Rue Riad El Moukha

Psge du Prince Moulay Rachid

14

Rue de la Recette

13

Rue Riad Zitoun El Kedim

31
27
29

Rue Riad Zitoun El Jedid

6
16
25
10

Dar Si Said

Musée Tiskiwin

2
11
3

Moroccan Arts Culinary Museum

Rue de la Bahia

Derb Jedid

26
30

Ave Houmane El Fetouaki

Rue Ibn Rachid

Rue Uqba Bin Nafaa

Rue Uqba Bin Nafaa

KASBAH

Rue Bab Mellah

Rue Bab el Mellah

MELLAH

Place des Ferblantiers

Rue de Berrima

Sights

Musée du Patrimoine Immatériel
MUSEUM

1 MAP P46, C4

Overlooking Djemaa El Fna, this museum celebrates the cultural aspects of Djemaa El Fna: the storytellers, acrobats, comedians, musicians and more through displays, film, photographs, music and art.

There are two paintings of the square by Jacques Majorelle. It is housed in the former national bank building, and also has a numismatic exhibition. (Museum of Intangible Heritage)

Musée Tiskiwin
MUSEUM

2 MAP P46, F6

Travel to Timbuktu and back again via the late Dutch anthropologist Bert Flint's art collection, crammed inside this ornate medina riad. Each room represents a caravan stop along the Sahara-to-Marrakesh route, presenting indigenous crafts from Tuareg camel saddles to High Atlas carpets.

The museum's displays and explanatory texts are eccentric, but Tiskiwin's well-travelled artefacts offer tantalising glimpses of Marrakesh's trading-post past. (tiskiwin.com)

Heritage Museum

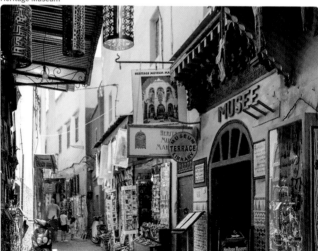

CHRIS GRIFFITHS/LONELY PLANET ©

Moroccan Culinary Arts Museum

MUSEUM

3 MAP P46, F6

Claiming to be the first of its kind in Morocco, this large riad museum should be the first stop in Marrakesh for food lovers. Set over three floors, exhibitions are neatly separated into different types of local cuisine, covering everything from soups to pastries and street food. English-language displays bring the history and culture surrounding Morocco's distinguished food heritage to life. Cooking classes are Dh600, and there's a restaurant (p51) on the rooftop. Book tickets online. (moroccan cam.com)

Heritage Museum

MUSEUM

4 MAP P46, E1

The Alouani Bibi family have thrown open the doors of this old riad to display their eclectic and fascinating collection of Moroccan artefacts. From Berber costumes and jewellery to minbars (mosque pulpits) and Roman amphorae, the exhibits (mostly labelled in English and French) cover the arc of Moroccan history and culture. The rooftop cafe is a tranquil spot amid the souq hustle. (Musée du Patrimoine)

Koutoubia Gardens

PARK

5 MAP P46, A5

Stretching out behind the Koutoubia Mosque, this palm-tree-dotted swathe of greenery

Assembly of the Dead

The meaning of Djemaa el Fna is shrouded in mystery. The 'Assembly of the Dead', the 'Mosque at the End of the World', and the 'Mosque of Ruination' have all been offered up by historians. In Arabic, *djemaa* can mean gathering, congregation, mosque or assembly. El Fna can mean the buried, the dead or the ruined. Those who argue for 'Assembly of the Dead' do so based on its past as the place of public execution. Others argue the name originates in a powerful 17th-century Saadian sultan's attempts to build a grand mosque on the site. His Mosque of Tranquillity was only partially built and so instead became known as the 'Mosque of Ruination'.

Recommended by Saeida Rouass,
writer and author of
Assembly of the Dead
@saeida.rouass

is a favourite Marrakshi spot for strolling, relaxing on park benches and generally taking a quiet break. If you need some downtime after dodging motorbikes amid the medina's skinny alleyways, take the locals' lead and head here for a peaceful meander. There are great views of the Koutoubia Mosque's minaret.

Eating

Mandala Society
FUSION $$

6 ⊗ MAP P46, F5

Brainchild of a Moroccan/Icelandic couple, this is a meat-free zone, though there is a lonely fish burger among all the vegetarian options. Share a sweet or savoury brunch board for two (Dh200), or anything with the sweet-potato fries. There are speciality teas and coffees, and delicious smoothies. It's a great vibe on the ground floor and roof terrace. (mandalasociety.com; 🖉)

Pepe Nero
ITALIAN $$$

7 ⊗ MAP P46, F4

Housed in part of Riad Al Moussika, Thami El Glaoui's one-time pleasure palace, this dreamy Italian-Moroccan restaurant is one of the finest in the medina. The showstealer is its fresh house-made

Film Festival

Marrakesh's long-running **International Film Festival** (festivalmarrakech.info) takes place every November. It gathers national and international filmmakers, actors and directors for special screenings and workshops at venues across the city, including the Musée Yves Saint Laurent. During the weeklong festival, film projections are beamed onto the Djemaa El Fna.

pasta, including imaginative veggie options like celeriac ravioli with chive sauce. Request a table beside the courtyard pool, rimmed by citrus trees, to make the most of the occasion. Reservations required (online). (pepenero-marrakech.com; 🛜🖉)

Naranj
LEBANESE $$

8 ⊗ MAP P46, F4

Naranj's ultraslick interior of *khamsa* (hand-shaped amulet) mirrors, low-hanging copper lamps and bar seating is quite a scene change on Riad Zitoun El Jedid. It wouldn't look out of place in a hipster 'hood in Beirut, which is the point, because the menu is a contemporary take on Lebanese. Head straight up to the lovely split-level terrace and order anything with falafel. (naranj.ma; 🛜🖉)

Cantine des Gazelles
MOROCCAN $$

9 ⊗ MAP P46, E3

All pink with straw hats and spilling out onto the pavement, this is a great place to eat with local and Mediterranean food. Try the beef tajine with prunes, apricots and almonds, or the chicken *tfaya* (a classic sweet and savoury dish). (instagram.com/lacantinedesgazelles)

La Famille
MEDITERRANEAN $$

10 ⊗ MAP P46, F5

Stepping through the alleyway into La Famille is like emerging through a Narnia wardrobe: it's a different

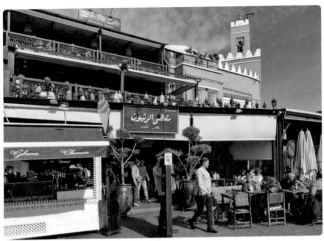

Zeitoun Cafe

world inside this leafy garden cafe, cocooned from the dusty souq outside. The wholesome menu is vegetarian, inventive and changes daily. Expect dishes like brussels-sprout gnocchi with parmesan, orange zest and dried fig, or barley salad with garlic cheese, salted chickpeas and pear. (📞 0524385295; 🛜 🖊️)

Museum of Culinary Arts Restaurant

MOROCCAN $$

Located on the rooftop at this lovely riad museum (see 3 📍 Map p46, F6), the restaurant serves classic Moroccan dishes. Outside of meal-times, you can have tea or lightly spiced coffee with Moroccan pastries. (moroccancam.com)

La Brillante

MOROCCAN $$$

11 🍴 MAP P46, F6

There are two restaurants at this ultra-modern hotel: La Terrasse on the rooftop serving a light Mediterranean menu, and the more formal La Table de Laila offering Moroccan classics with a twist. Weekend brunches (including use of the pool) are Dh650. Enjoy a glass of wine at La Terrasse bar with its splendid mountain and medina views. (h-labrillante.com)

Zeitoun Cafe

MOROCCAN $$

12 🍴 MAP P46, D3

This family-friendly restaurant has the loveliest tiered terraces on the Djemaa. Honest Moroccan cooking and panoramic views over

Mechoui Alley

🍽️

Just before noon, the vendors at this row of **stalls** (Map p46, D2) start carving up steaming sides of *mechoui* (slow-roasted lamb). Very little English is spoken, but simply point to the best-looking cut of meat, and ask for a *nus* (half) or *rubb* (quarter) kilo. The cook will hack off falling-from-the-bone lamb and hand it to you with fresh-baked bread, cumin and salt. Choose to take away or eat in at benches behind the counter, beside the hot hole in the floor where the lamb is cooked.

The alley's southern entrance is most famous for **Chez Lahmine Hadj Mustapha** (Map p46, D3). The speciality here is the paper-sealed crockpots of *tanjia*, Morocco's famed 'bachelor's stew'. Use bread as your utensil to scoop up the butter-soft meat.

the square make it perfect for lingering. The kids' menu (Dh50) and hot milk with orange blossom will keep little ones happy, and there's a *tanjia de chameau*, a camel meat take on Marrakesh's speciality dish, for adventurous diners. (zeitouncafe.com; 📶👶)

Marrakech Henna Art Cafe

CAFE $

13 ❌ MAP P46, D5

This charming cafe and gallery with rooftop terraces has a vegetarian- and vegan-conscious menu serving a mix of North African dishes, sandwiches, wraps and salads (the Berber omelette is a winner). True to its name, it also has local art exhibits, a collection of Amazigh artefacts, wall murals and the op- portunity to get your own piece of henna body art (from Dh50). (marrakechhennaartcafe.com; 📶✏️)

Pâtisserie des Princes

PASTRIES $

14 ❌ MAP P46, C5

This is one of the city's most famous patisseries, with enough petits fours to keep Marrakesh dentists in business. Its ice cream is one of the best around and comes in Moroccan flavours such as date, fig and orange. The small cafe at the back is a welcome respite for women. (📞0524443033)

Café Kessabine

MOROCCAN $

15 ❌ MAP P46, E2

Snuggled in the northeastern cor- ner of Djemaa El Fna, with terraces across two different sites opposite each other, the Kessabine may not have the panoramic views of some other cafes, but it makes up for that with a chilled-out, slightly bohemian vibe. All the Moroc- can classics are present: tajines, *briouats* (fried savoury stuffed pastries), *brochettes* (kebabs) and couscous. There are also tacos and chips. (📞0636429369; 🖥)

Un Déjeuner à Marrakech   MEDITERRANEAN $$

16 ❌ MAP P46, F5

Popular with the lunching crowd, Un Déjeuner serves up a Mediterranean-Moroccan fusion menu that jumps from monkfish with thyme butter, caramelised potato, baked eggplant and pumpkin with lemon confit gravy, to a very fancy burger. Dishes are unusually refined, and the cactus-lined roof terrace is the place to be with a glass of wine on a breezy blue-sky Moroccan day. (📞0524378387; 🖥🗡)

Drinking

Kabana   ROOFTOP BAR

17 🍺 MAP P46, A3

It feels like there's a bit of Bali and a bit of Senegal in this lively yet relaxed rooftop bar with views of Koutoubia Mosque. Vintage furniture, natural materials and palm prints give the terrace a chic boho feel. Staff give out blankets on colder nights, and there's indoor seating beneath a forest of lanterns for rainy days. Try the signature travel-themed cocktails. (kabana-marrakech.com; 🖥)

Café El Koutoubia   CAFE

18 🍺 MAP P46, A4

The street terrace at this charmingly old-fashioned cafe with

Les Jardins de la Koutoubia (p54)

Best Rooftop Djemaa Views

To truly appreciate the size and drama of Djemaa El Fna, you need to see it from a roof terrace. But which one?

Grand Balcon du Café Glacier (Map p46, D4) Perfectly poised for viewing both sides of the square.

Zeitoun Cafe (p51) The overlook with the best food.

Taj'in Darna (Map p46, D4; tajindarna.com; 📶) Serves the cheapest breakfast (from Dh45) and has good service.

Café de France (Map p46, D3) An institution, but always crammed, prices are high and service is often poor.

wrought-iron balustrades has cracking views of the Koutoubia minaret across the road. Despite its touristy position, it's a favourite hang out for both elderly gentlemen clad in *djellaba* (traditional hooded robes) – plus suited businessmen – plus the occasional Marrakshi hipster – giving it a properly local ambience.

Le Salama   BAR

19 🚇 MAP P46, D3

You might not be able to see the Djemaa El Fna from Le Salama's light-filled 'sky bar', but the 360-degree views from its floor-to-ceiling windows make up for it, particularly with a sundowner in hand. With Middle Eastern beats and trailing foliage hanging from the roof, it's a surprisingly atmospheric place for drinks. Bonus: happy hour (two-for-one) runs virtually all day. (facebook.com/lesalamamarrakech; 📶)

Les Jardins de la Koutoubia   BAR

20 🚇 MAP P46, B3

This 1920s hotel offers drinkers double trouble. At sunset, head straight up to the Sky Bar, a secret haven of stylish, shady day beds and trickling fountains, with a shisha menu. When night falls, move downstairs into the classiest gin joint in the medina, with powerful long drinks delivered to leather club chairs beneath cedar ceilings.

To find the Sky Bar, take the lift in the northwest corner (behind the pool) up to the 3rd floor. (les jardinsdelakoutoubia.com)

Café Semmarine   CAFE

21 🚇 MAP P46, D1

This old-fashioned cafe with its wooden stained-glass entranceway is hidden right inside bustling Rue Semmarine. Inside it's spotlessly clean, and the teeny front terrace is an engrossing spot to watch stallholders and their customers as you sip one of the best coffees you'll find in the souqs.

Kafé Fnaque Berbère CAFE

22 🚇 MAP P46, C2

Sadly the bookstore that made this cafe unique is no more, but Fnaque Berbère still has efficient staff and one of the highest bird's-eye views of the medina's souqs from what must be the dinkiest terrace in Marrakesh. The food is average, but it's a great place for a tea break. (📞0649583165)

Bakchich CAFE

23 🚇 MAP P46, E3

This laid-back spot with outdoor seating under a bright yellow awning is a good choice to chill after weaving through the souqs. Grab one of the tables, order a juice and watch the alleyway traffic pass by. There's a decent menu of salads and tajines (Dh55 to Dh75) if you're feeling peckish.

Local Hassle & Getting Lost

Marrakesh's **tourist police** (Brigade Touristique; Map p46, C3; 📞0524384601) have, in recent years, managed to stymie the worst of the city's hustler problem – particularly faux guides – but not completely eliminate it. The Kâat Ben Nahid neighbourhood is an area where tourists may still experience persistent hassle – beware of the local teenage boys, some of whom are pickpockets and will target those who look lost.

○ Know that official guides wear a lanyard with their photograph and registration number. It's extremely rare to see them touting for business on the streets.

○ Be aware that a hustler's main interest is usually gaining commission from the restaurant, hotel or shop that they have guided you to.

○ If you are lost in the medina, ask a shopkeeper for directions. Often bored youths will point you in the wrong direction on purpose.

○ If you employ an unofficial guide to help you get somewhere in the medina (usually to Djemaa El Fna), a tip of a few dirham will suffice.

○ GPS technology can now just about cope with the medina architecture. Google Maps is decent (except in the central souqs) but Maps.Me is better; download offline maps so you have them when roaming is switched off.

○ Generally it's fine to have your phone out in the medina, but if locals tell you to put it away (which does sometimes happen), do heed their advice.

Appropriate Medina Attire ⓘ

In Gueliz shorts and tank tops are fine, but in the medina, where life remains more traditional, your choice of attire may be perceived as a sign of respect for yourself and Moroccans alike.

For both men and women, this means not wearing shorts, sleeveless tops or revealing clothing. If you do, some people will be embarrassed for you and the family that raised you and will avoid eye contact. So if you don't want to miss out on some excellent company – especially among older Moroccans – dress modestly.

Riad Yima   TEAHOUSE

24 🚇 MAP P46, D2

Acclaimed Moroccan artist and photographer Hassan Hajjaj created this kitsch-crammed tearoom, boutique and gallery. Here, all your preconceived notions of Moroccan restaurants and riads, with their *Arabian Nights* fantasy of candlelit lanterns, arches and belly dancers, are revamped with a tongue-in-cheek sense of humour, accompanied by a traditional glass of mint tea, of course. It's signposted from Rahba Kedima.

Shopping

Naturom   COSMETICS

25 🔒 MAP P46, F5

Naturom's neatly packaged and keenly priced argan, verbena, fig or orange-blossom beauty products are all 100% certified organic, using pure essences and essential oils. With its own medicinal and herbal garden, it has full traceability of most raw materials. Staff speak excellent English and can guide you through the range, including anti-ageing prickly pear oil and hammam *gommage* (exfoliating scrub). (☎0524383784)

Jad   COSMETICS

26 🔒 MAP P46, E7

Want to take home the Zen aroma of Marrakesh's riads and spas? Jad has captured evocative local scents such as orange blossom, fig, black and green tea, and poured them into its stylish range of Le Sens de Marrakech bath products, room mists and diffusers, all made in Marrakesh. (☎0524428737)

Les Marrisiennes   FASHION & ACCESSORIES

27 🔒 MAP P46, E6

Moroccan embroidery is a signature of Les Marrisiennes' Parisian-designed, Marrakesh-made fashions, but there's nothing traditional about these pieces, which take Moroccan icons such as *babouches* (leather slippers) and fez hats and turn them into patterns for floaty skirts and loose shirts. Designer Chloe Place produces two limited collections a year, bringing a mix of fun prints and simple, contemporary Moroccan style in her medina shop. (☏0661509527)

Aromatimri COSMETICS

28 MAP P46, E3

Aromatimri has been around since 1968, making cosmetics using local plants. This gorgeous little shop sells 100% natural, organic oils and essential oils, including argan oil and prickly-pear oil. The face creams, soaps, massage oils, serums and *ghassouls* (clay masks) are all beautifully packaged. (aromatimri.com)

Yannass HOMEWARES

29 MAP P46, E6

This upmarket concept store is a sign of the times on gentrifying Riad Zitoun El Kedim. Its walls are lined with shelves of beautifully packaged saffron, local jams and essential oils, artfully arranged beside black-and-white KAM Design ceramic teapots, bowls and mugs. Contemplate your purchases at the communal table with a cup of Marrakesh's Bloom coffee, brewed behind the counter. (☏0653052255)

Wafl Design DESIGN

30 MAP P46, E7

Bold, colourful and tongue-in-cheek: Wafl's Belgian-designed pop-art illustrations are part

Riad Yima

CHRIS GRIFFITHS/LONELY PLANET ©

of a new art vanguard in Marrakesh that's eschewing traditional Moroccan design tropes. There are kitsch homewares, such as 'Marrakesh Starbucks' mugs, but it's the clever illustrations that are most striking, such as a camel cocking a leg on a palm tree and cans of Camel's Couscous Soup – a spin on Andy Warhol's *Campbell's Soup Cans*. (facebook.com/wafldesign)

Akéwa
FASHION & ACCESSORIES

31 📍 MAP P46, E6

French-Gabonese fashion designer François imports his wax-print fabrics directly from Gabon, Ivory Coast, Senegal and Mali to make bold contemporary African clothing. The breezy skirts, tailored suits and tees are all machine washable and look all the more striking for being displayed against an all-black shop interior. (📞0629772652)

Souq Ableuh
FOOD

32 📍 MAP P46, D3

Swerve off Djemaa El Fna to this tiny souq dedicated to olives. Green olives, black olives, purple olives, and olives marinated in *harissa* (hot chilli paste) – it's basically olive heaven.

Warda La Mouche
FASHION & ACCESSORIES

33 📍 MAP P46, E4

Those after a touch of Moroccan boho-chic style will love Warda La Mouche's floaty sundresses with quirky embroidery detail,

Carpets for sale

Carpet Buying for Beginners

Rabati Plush pile carpets in deep jewel tones, featuring an ornate central motif balanced by fine border details. Rabati carpets are highly prized and could run to Dh2000 per sq metre.

Chichaoua Simple and striking, with zigzags, asterisks and enigmatic symbols on a variegated red or purple background (about Dh700 to Dh1000 per sq metre).

Hanbels or kilims These are flat weaves with no pile. Some *hanbels* include Tifinagh (Berber) letters and auspicious symbols such as the evil eye, Southern Cross and Berber *fibule* (brooch) in their weave (about Dh700 to Dh900 per sq metre).

Zanafi or glaoua Kilims and shag carpeting, together at last. Opposites attract in these rugs, where sections of fluffy pile alternate with flat-woven stripes or borders. These are usually Dh1000 to Dh1750 per sq metre.

Shedwi Flat weaves with bold patterns in black wool on off-white. For as little as Dh400 for a smaller rug, they make impressive yet inexpensive gifts.

summery tops with post-hippie flair and sophisticated harem pants. It's all handmade (but machine washable), designed in Marrakesh by French shop owner Sandrine. (☎ 0524389063)

Funduq El Ouarzazi
ARTS & CRAFTS

35 🔒 MAP P46, C2

This slightly decrepit *funduq* (inn once used by caravans) is a dream come true for shoppers who enjoy poking about in pursuit of treasure as much as the actual buying. Around 40 cubby-hole shops have claimed space over two floors; a clutter of traditional jewellery,

Amazigh artefacts and dusty antiques. Accept a mint tea from the shopkeepers and hunt away.

Art Ouarzazate
FASHION & ACCESSORIES

35 🔒 MAP P46, E2

Tried and tested techniques in weaving, leather work and embroidery are transformed into high-fashion dandy jackets, *djellaba*-inspired velvet capes and boho patterned dresses by dynamic duo Samad and Malek. Beyond the '70s-inspired clothes racks, there are oversized leather totes, *babouches* and horn jewellery to covet. (☎ 0648584833)

Explore ◉

Mouassine & Central Souqs

The lanes that spool north from Djemaa El Fna sum up the push and pull between old and new in Marrakesh. This atmospheric area is home to the city's biggest concentration of souqs and qissariat, but then you hit Mouassine where a fresh breed of boutiques, Mediterranean-inspired rooftop restaurants and lounge-style cafes are shaking up the medina.

The Short List

○ **Le Jardin Secret (p66)** *Taking a souq chill pill at these historic Islamic gardens, irrigated by traditional waterworks.*

○ **Musée de la Musique (p69)** *Exploring the exhibits and architectural finery of this Saadian-era riad.*

○ **Rahba Kedima (p63)** *Soaking up the atmosphere on this gentrifying square with lively apothecaries, designer shops and rooftop cafes.*

○ **Nomad (p71)** *Catching the breeze on the waterfall terraces at this buzzy restaurant that has spurred a revolution in medina dining.*

○ **Hammams (p66)** *Scrubbing, steaming and soaking it up – either at a characterful spa or in public Hammam Mouassine.*

Getting There & Around

🚶 The best route north from Djemaa El Fna is to take Souq Semmarine up to Place Rahba Kedima and beyond.

🚗 There is no car access through the souqs. Convenient drop-off gateways are Bab Laksour and Dar El Bacha.

Neighbourhood Map on p64

Rahba Kedima (p63) CKTRAVELS.COM/SHUTTERSTOCK ©

Walking Tour 🚶

Discovering the Heart of the Souqs

The very core of Marrakesh is a medley of buying, selling, haggling and hawking, but it's not all about carpets, ceramics and twinkly lamps – although, yes you'll find those as well. Here you'll see metalworkers busy at their trade, apothecaries with tiny shops full of exotic herbal remedies and Marrakshis doing their shopping at hole-in-the-wall butcher shops and vegetable carts.

Walk Facts

Start & End Place Rahba Kedima

Length 1.5km; two hours

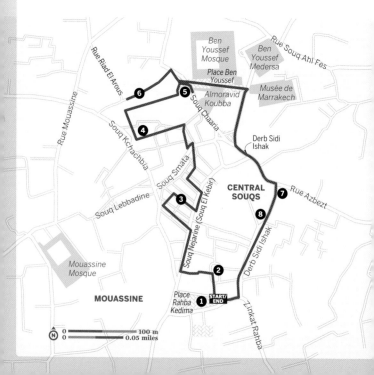

❶ Spice Action at Rahba Kedima

Begin your stroll in **Place Rahba Kedima**, a square rimmed by spice stores. Moroccans use their local spice stall as a one-stop shop for natural remedies to cure sickness and ailments, and potions to eliminate mischievous *jinn* (spirits) as well as to pep up their cooking. The square's also recently become a hotbed for local designers.

❷ Carpet Souq

It's hard to believe that **Souk de Tapis** once functioned as Marrakesh's main slave market, where the human cargo of the caravan trade were bought and sold. Carpet auctions are held around 4pm to 5pm (after the afternoon prayer) every day except Friday: look for the sign 'Le Souk Principal de Tapis'.

❸ Into the Qissariat

The zigzagging alleys that lie between Souq Nejarine and Souq Smata are the *qissariat* (covered markets). Although tourist-focused shops have moved in, this is still a local haunt crammed with *djellabas* (hooded garments with long sleeves) and *babouches* (leather slippers).

❹ Blacksmiths at Work

Souq Haddadine (p76), the Blacksmith's Market, is full of busy workshops where the sound of the metalworkers' hammers provides a staccato background beat. You'll find grimy welders and mechanics here, as well as craftspeople making decorative items.

❺ A Local Lunch

Behind Souq Haddadine, the blacksmith clanging is replaced by the sizzle of grilled meat. The **Ben Youssef Food Stalls** serve up meat skewers, and the occasional stewed sheep's head, to a lunchtime crew of hungry market workers. Pull up a pew and eat whatever looks fresh.

❻ Leather-Hide Workshops

Take a stroll in the leatherworker's alley nearby where the stalls are piled high with leather hides ready to be turned into handbags and shoes. During morning hours you can often see freshly dyed leather hides left out to dry in the sun in Place Ben Youssef.

❼ Central Vegetable Market

Locals come here wielding their baskets to stock up on fruit, herbs and fresh local produce that's laid out at stalls and upon blankets on the cobblestones. For a snack, pick up some fruit here; haggling isn't necessary.

❽ Butcher's Alley

The lane through the arch leading south from the vegetable market is lined with small butcher's stores. Check out the entrails, offal and swinging carcasses as you walk through back to Rahba Kedima.

0
0
200 m
0.1 miles

For reviews see
⊙ Sights   p66
✕ Eating   p70
☕ Drinking   p73
🔒 Shopping   p74

Derb Tizeguarine

Arset Aouzal

Rue Dar El Ghiaour

Rue Dar El Bacha

Hammam de la Rose
⊙ 8

Dar El Bacha
3 ⊙ ☕17

Rue Dar El Bacha

Funduq El Amri

DAR EL BACHA

35 🔒

16 ✕
Derb Chorfa Lakbir
☕32

Rue Sidi El Yamani

☕ 22

Le Bain Bleu ⊙ 7

Rue Sidi El Yamani

26 🔒

Rue Laksour

☕18

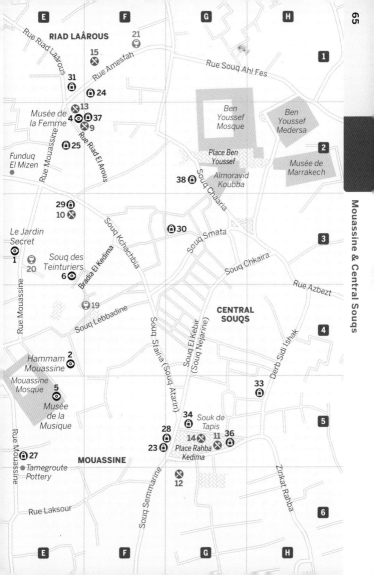

RIAD LAÂROUS

Rue Riad Laârous

Rue Amesfah

21

15

31

24

Rue Souq Ahl Fes

Musée de la Femme

13

4 37

9

25

Rue Mouassine

Rue Riad El Arous

Funduq El Mizen

Ben Youssef Mosque

Ben Youssef Medersa

Place Ben Youssef

Musée de Marrakech

Almoravid Koubba

38

Souq Chaaria

29

10

Le Jardin Secret

1

Souq Kchachbia

30

Souq Smata

Souq Chkaira

Rue Azbezt

Souq des Teinturiers

20

6

Bradia El Kedima

19

Souq Lebbadine

Rue Mouassine

CENTRAL SOUQS

Souq Stalia (Souq Atarin)

Souq El Kebir (Souq Nejarine)

Derb Sidi L'Ishak

Hammam Mouassine

2

Mouassine Mosque

5

Musée de la Musique

33

27

Tamegroute Pottery

34

Souk de Tapis

MOUASSINE

28

23

14 11 36

Place Rahba Kedima

12

Souq Semmarine

Zinkat Rahba

Rue Laksour

Sights

Le Jardin Secret

MUSEUM

1  MAP P64, E3

The foundations of this historic riad are more than 400 years old, and it was once owned by powerful *qaid* (local chief) U-Bihi. Here, though, it's not the building but the traditional Islamic garden that is so special. Fed by a restored original *khettara* (underground irrigation system), the gardens are set up as a living museum to demonstrate the ancient waterworks. There's a good **cafe** on its ramparts and a tower with views across the medina. (lejardinsecret marrakech.com)

Hammam Mouassine

HAMMAM

2  MAP P64, E4

A proper public hammam that also caters for travellers looking for an authentic experience. In business since 1562, Hammam Mouassine has charming and professional staff who will wash you and then scrub you down (*gommage*) with Morocco's famed *rhassoul* clay until you're squeaky clean (Dh150). As with other public hammams, you could also DIY it here and pay just the entrance fee.

This is one of the few public hammams with English-speaking reception staff, who will furnish you with a bag for your belongings and a disposable mitt for your hammam. Men enter the hammam through the marked archway

Le Jardin Secret

SERENITY H./SHUTTERSTOCK ©

Thami El Glaoui: Marrakesh's Pasha Warlord

Rumoured to be one of the richest men in the world in the mid-20th century, Thami El Glaoui was the ruler who kept Marrakesh under lock and key during the French protectorate years. He was an Atlas Mountain warlord who controlled the rich desert trade routes. Machiavellian manoeuvring and a fearsome reputation for ruling with an iron fist brought him to the French, who effectively handed Marrakesh to Glaoui from 1912 to 1956. He helped depose Sultan Mohammed V, a decision he would live to regret as the sultan eventually returned to power.

Glaoui died in disgrace in January 1956, two months before Moroccan independence. Yet his name is still writ large across the city – his greatest epitaph is his palace, Dar El Bacha, built in the early 20th century. Up until the early 1950s, severed heads sometimes garnished the palace walls.

Glaoui was a man of contradictions; a lover of the limelight who graced parties in London and Paris, loved jazz and invited celebrities such as Charlie Chaplin, Edith Piaf and Josephine Baker to Marrakesh during the 1920s and '30s (Baker was even said to be his lover). Meanwhile, behind palace walls, he had a harem of 150 women and an entourage of slaves. His life is the subject of the highly regarded book *Lords of the Atlas* (1966) by Gavin Maxwell.

on the east side of Mouassine Fountain. The women's entrance is through the signposted alleyway on the west side.

Dar El Bacha   MUSEUM

3 ◉ MAP P64, A2

This palace was built for Pacha Thami El Glaoui, also known as the Lord of the Atlas, who ruled over Marrakesh from 1912 to 1956. It is one of the medina's finest examples of riad architecture, dripping with *zellige* (colourful geometric tilework), intricate white plasterwork and heavy carved cedar-wood lintels, and opened to the public in 2015 as the Museum of Confluences. Well-presented exhibitions, which inhabit the salons around the main courtyard, span the arts and change around every six months. (Museum of Confluences; https://darbacha.com/)

Musée de la Femme   MUSEUM

4 ◉ MAP P64, E2

Spread over three floors, Marrakesh's Museum of Women was launched in 2018 by a passionate bunch of locals intent on championing women's important role in Moroccan society. The museum completely reinvents itself with a

Hammam
How-To

(i)

Want to find all the locals in the medina? Get thee to the public hammam. Every neighbourhood has one, and these institutions have served as the nexus of city communities in Morocco for centuries. Some public hammams are unmarked, and others simply have a picture of a man or woman stencilled on the wall outside. For some top picks see p18. Note that some hammams don't accept non-Muslims – ask inside.

What to Take

○ You'll need a hammam kit of towel, flip-flops and a plastic mat (to sit on), as well as a spare pair of underwear and your shampoo and soap.

○ You can also bring your own Moroccan *savon beldi* (black soap made from the resin of olives), *kessa* (coarse scrubbing mitt), and *ghassoul* (clay mixed with herbs, dried roses and lavender): buy them from the souqs, or in the fancier beauty stores.

What to Expect

Nudity is common in some public hammams, but local etiquette differs between neighbourhoods: if unsure, ask an attendant what the done thing is. Some may ask both men and women to keep their underpants on; bras are less common. However, it's always perfectly acceptable to wear your swimsuit if this makes you feel more comfortable.

○ Entry costs about Dh10, with optional massage for Dh50 to Dh100. Pay at a counter near the door and then move into the changing area, where you may be asked to pay an extra few dirhams if you want attendants to watch your possessions. Attendants usually speak minimal English.

○ There are three stages to a typical hammam – wash, scrub and massage. You'll be given a bucket and scoop, which you fill with water from the communal tap.

○ Find a space on the floor (this is where your plastic mat comes in handy) and sluice yourself down.

○ Now it's time for a scrub. If you're in do-it-yourself mode, you'll have brought along a *kessa*, or you can pay a hammam attendant for a vigorous *gommage* (scrub).

new exhibition every six months, and past themes have included modern female pioneers and tribal fashions and their influence on global design. (Museum of Women; museedelafemme.ma)

Musée de la Musique   MUSEUM

5 ⊙ MAP P64, E5

While house-hunting in the medina, Parisian Patrick Menac'h stumbled across a historic treasure of great cultural significance. Beneath the layers of white plaster of a modest riad's 1st-floor *douiria* (guest apartment) was a jewel of domestic Saadian architecture from the 1560s. The riad's ground-floor rooms hold a small collection of Amazigh artefacts and temporary photography exhibitions, but the painstakingly restored interior of the upstairs salons are where concerts are held. There's also a small rooftop **cafe**.

The other major projects of this period, when the Saadians were busy transforming Marrakesh into their imperial capital, are all grand in scale – the mosques at Mouassine, Bab Doukkala, Ben Youssef and Sidi Bel Abbes. But this bijou 1st-floor *douiria* was created by a *chorfa* (noble) family after the Saadians relocated the Mouassine Jews to the *mellah* (Jewish quarter) and gave the city a new dynamic. The *douiria,* in its restored form, is thus an important example of domestic architecture in this era and a commentary on the courtly art of hospitality. Imagine the

mindset of travel-weary guests as they entered the main salon with its symphony of colour: verdigris and apricot climb the walls in a vertical garden, while bedrooms are trimmed with sculpted Kufic script framed by azure blue and finished with a fine Pompeiian red skirting. You may assume the vivid colours on show are the work of the 24-man restoration team, but the decor is, amazingly, original – their vibrancy preserved beneath layers of plaster for centuries. In the side salon, you can view a fascinating short video of some of the restoration methods. Menac'h, who set up the museum, is also behind Maison de la Photographie (p84). (Musée de Mouassine; museedemouassine.com)

Souq des Teinturiers   MARKET

6 ⊙ MAP P64, E3

The dyers souq is one of Marrakesh's most colourful markets, with skeins of coloured wool draped from the rafters above stalls. However, very little remains of its original purpose. Seek out shop number 19 (there's a sign above the doorway, but it may be partially obscured), which has the souq's only remaining dying vat inside the door, still stained with indigo.

Le Bain Bleu   SPA

7 ⊙ MAP P64, D6

Relaxation pools are usually reserved for Marrakesh's luxury spas, but Le Bain Bleu sets itself apart from the competition with

Marrakesh's Fanadiq

Fanadiq (inns once used by caravans – the singular is *funduq*) once dotted the important stopover towns on Morocco's caravan routes. Since medieval times, these creative courtyard complexes provided ground-floor stables and workshops, and rented rooms for desert traders and travelling merchants upstairs, and from this flux of artisans and adventurers emerged the inventive culture of modern-day Marrakesh. As trading communities became more stable and affluent, though, most *fanadiq* were gradually replaced with private homes and storehouses.

Only 140 *fanadiq* remain in the medina, many of them now converted into artisan complexes. Most retain shreds of fine original woodcarving, romantic balconies and even some stucco work, and there has been a recent drive to restore them, part of a citywide push to upgrade historic sites. The best to poke your head into to admire their well-travelled, shop-worn glory are found on Rue Dar El Bacha and Rue Mouassine; try **Funduq El Amri** (Map p64, D2) and **Funduq El Mizen** (Map p64, E2).

a lovely lounging pool courtyard, as well as a rooftop for post-pampering sun snoozes, airy petal-strewn rest room and rooftop bar-restaurant called **Dar Justo**. Couples hammam packages, facials, manicures and pedicures are available. It's well signposted off Rue El Mouassine. (lebainbleu.com)

Hammam de la Rose SPA

8 ◉ MAP P64, C2

This atmospheric private hammam gets the thumbs-up for its superprofessional staff and squeaky-clean premises. There's a range of beauty treatments you can add, from rose facial masks and clay cleansing to a host of massage options. (hammamdelarose.com)

Eating

Le Jardin MOROCCAN $$

9 ✕ MAP P64, F2

Entrepreneur Kamal Laftimi transformed this 17th-century riad in the medina's core into a contemporary, oh-so-pretty oasis where you can lunch beneath a canopy of banana trees, serenaded by songbirds, as tiny tortoises inch across the floor tiles. The menu's modern edge shines through in dishes like Agadir octopus with romesco sauce and fish fillet with preserved lemon sauce. Booking recommended. (https://lejardin marrakech.com; 📶 ✐)

Terrasse des Épices

MOROCCAN $$$

10  MAP P64, E3

Lazy, hazy Mediterranean ambience is guaranteed at this hip rooftop above Souq Cherifia, where beautiful people gather in booths for chilled beats and accomplished Moroccan or global dishes chalked up on blackboards. It's one of the few places in this part of the medina where you can order wine or beer alongside dishes like Caesar salad or lobster rice with *tanjia* sauce. (terrassedesepices.com; 📷)

Ayaso

MEDITERRANEAN $$

11  MAP P64, G5

Bright, modern restaurant with a tall terrace overlooking the square. Come by for breakfast *bissara* (fava-bean and garlic soup with cumin, olive oil and a dash of paprika; Dh4O) as the market wakes up, or tuck into the freshest organic salads sprinkled with spirulina and sprouts. The Indian chicken curry with naan and salad (Dh105) is recommended. Many ingredients are grown on a farm in Ourika. Honey, saffron and other health products are for sale. Look them up on Instagram #ayaso.bio. (📞0808660938)

Nomad

MEDITERRANEAN $$

12  MAP P64, G6

Nomad's multitiered rooftop is one of the medina's buzziest venues, particularly at night when its lanterns twinkle over Rahba Kedima. The small menu adds contemporary twists to North

Terrasse des Épices

African ingredients and flavours, creating dishes such as Agadir calamari in a cumin-infused anchovy sauce or spiced lamb burger with smoky aubergine. Vegetarian and vegan dishes, like cauliflower roasted with *chermoula* and harissa, are excellent. (nomad marrakech.com; 🛜🍴)

Souk Kafé   MOROCCAN $$

13 🍽 MAP P64, E2

Climb to the rooftop, doff your sunhat to the giant rattan teapot and plonk down on a cushion ready to stay a while: this is authentic local food worth savouring. The Moroccan mezze of six cooked vegetable dishes qualifies as lunch for two – but wait until you get a whiff of the aromatic Marrakshi *tanjia*, with its slow-cooked, perfectly falling-apart beef. (📞0664172456; 🛜🚻)

Café des Épices   CAFE $

14 🍽 MAP P64, G5

A traveller's institution with a big open front, parked in prime position on Rahba Kedima (p63). Watch the henna artists and basket sellers tout for business while munching on a sardine ball tajine or a kefta sandwich and sipping a fresh fruit juice. Try to get a seat on the upper terrace to dodge the motorcycle fumes. (📞0524391770)

Soul Food by Le 14   FUSION $$

15 🍽 MAP P64, F1

Design duo Jan Pauwels and Salah-eddine have opened this multilevel colourful rooftop terrace

View from Café des Épices

The Making of Marrakesh

The Amazigh Sanhaja tribe founded the Almoravid dynasty in the 11th century and swept through the south of Morocco, demolishing opponents as they rode north. They pitched their campsite on a desolate swathe of land that would become Marrakesh. Amazigh Almoravid leader Youssef ben Tachfine and his savvy wife Zeinab recognised its strategic potential, and built ramparts around the encampment in 1062 CE. The Almoravids established the city's *khettara* (underground irrigation canals) and signature pink mudbrick architecture. At the age of almost 80, Youssef ben Tachfine launched successful campaigns securing Almoravid control of Andalucia. Marrakesh, once just a patch of dirt, became the operational centre of an empire that stretched right up to Barcelona's city limits.

above their flagship medina Different. (p75) concept store with cosy nooks, boho rattan lighting and Berber-style banquette seating under big parasols. The menu is an eclectic mashup of pizza, quinoa salads and Moroccan dishes that use artistic licence, including an ingenious *tanjia*-spiced beef fillet with chunky chips. (📞0524427645)

La Table du Palais   MEDITERRANEAN $$$

16 🍽 MAP P64, D4

Nothing beats a palm-shaded lunch or candle-lit dinner after a hectic medina day, and this extremely pretty courtyard restaurant delivers on peaceful ambience. The menus cherry-pick French and Moroccan influences, creating a Mediterranean fusion. Good meal deals can help keep costs down, and there's a jazzy little bar for a nightcap. (palaislamrani.com; 📶)

Drinking

Bacha Coffee   CAFE

17 🍵 MAP P64, B2

Tucked within the chambers of the Dar El Bacha museum (p67), this fancy salon cafe brings coffee connoisseurship back to Marrakesh. Prepare to scrape your jaw off the floor when you see the opulent rooms (a throwback to the early 20th-century French-protectorate era), the 23-page menu of 100% arabica coffees and the prices (pot of coffee from Dh44).

El Fenn   COCKTAIL BAR

18 🍵 MAP P64, B6

The best place to see the Koutoubia Mosque's nightly illumination is this achingly hip rooftop bar set up by Richard Branson's sister. Here, Marrakesh's movers and shakers converge for the medina's best cocktails and relaxed DJ sets.

Skip the disappointing, overpriced restaurant, but do plan for an evening sipping martinis under cushion-strewn Berber tents. (el-fenn.com; 🛜)

Terrasse des Teinturiers
CAFE

19 🚇 MAP P64, F4

Souqs exhausting you? Climb up the stairs to find a little rooftop oasis high above the haggling din, with colourful skeins of wool hanging from the rooftop pagoda. There's ultra-refreshing mint tea, cold juice and coffee, as well as tajines and couscous (from Dh75) if you're hungry. (📞0524391252)

Café Arabe
BAR

20 🚇 MAP P64, E3

Gloat over souq purchases with cocktails on the roof of this bar-restaurant popular with artists, designers and expats. Prices are reasonable for such a stylish place, and you can order half bottles of decent Moroccan wines. The rooftop is divided into two sections, one reserved for diners (Italian cuisine as well as Moroccan), the other for drinkers. (cafearabe.com; 🛜)

Atay Cafe
CAFE

21 🚇 MAP P64, F1

There's a striking Mediterranean-island vibe on this cute cafe's rooftop, which is all rattan shades and white-cane furniture, but the music plants Atay firmly in Africa. It's a pleasant place to hang out, idle over a fresh juice or breakfast, or test out the tasty tajines (from Dh75). (📞0661344246; 🛜)

Dar Cherifa
CAFE

22 🚇 MAP P64, D5

Ring the doorbell to be admitted into this serene 16th-century Saadian riad. Tea, juice and spiced Moroccan coffee are served on ultracomfy yellow armchairs in a courtyard framed by soaring sandstone pillars topped with intricate cedar lintels. Surrounding salons are home to art exhibitions. Meals can be underwhelming, but the jazz-enhanced atmosphere is quite dreamy. (📞0524426463; 🛜)

Shopping

Sissi Morocco
FASHION & ACCESSORIES

23 🔒 MAP P64, F5

This memorable Marrakesh brand has taken old sepia photos of Amazigh tribal women and incorporated them into hand-embroidered and printed bolster cushions, tote bags, purses and t-shirts. The results are striking, and the quality is top notch. French designer Silvie Pissard has her main boutique in Sidi Ghanem, but this petite branch is more conveniently located. (sissimorocco.com)

Different. FASHION & ACCESSORIES

24 🔒 MAP P64, F1

Brace yourself for the future of Marrakesh: Belgian-Moroccan design duo Jan Pauwels and Salah-eddine have taken over multiple premises to create this giant temple to contemporary Moroccan design. One side is all about quirky jewellery, colour-pop ceramics, posters and cheeky slogan t-shirts, while the other features jazzy caftans, slouchy active-wear and outrageously embellished jackets that wouldn't look out of place on the catwalk. (📞0524375570)

Kitan CLOTHING

25 🔒 MAP P64, E2

Upmarket boutique featuring clothing and accessories in excellent fabrics. Local artisans offer bespoke pieces all overseen by Japanese-born designer Mae Yamazak. (www.instagram.com/kitan_marrakech)

Al Nour ARTS & CRAFTS

26 🔒 MAP P64, C6

This smart cooperative run by local women with disabilities is where you can find fabulous neutral household linens, embroidered garments and top-quality accessories. All the textiles can be made to measure, and it's a popular place for stylish hand-stitched Marrakesh-mod tunics, dresses and shirts for men, women and kids. Purchases pay for salaries, training programmes and healthcare. (alnour-textiles.com)

36 Mouassine Concept Store DESIGN

27 🔒 MAP P64, E5

A paradise of all things design-related: bags and hats, clothing, *objets*, lamps, furniture and

Tamegroute Pottery

Recognisable by its vivid green glaze the colour of desert palms, Tamegroute pottery comes from a town in southern Morocco just before the landscape morphs into the Sahara. Its design cred has soared recently thanks to its appearance in high-end homewares shops abroad, and sellers have begun to pop up in Marrakesh. Several shops around town sell it, but the **stall** (Map p64, E6; 📞0662084871) on Rue Mouassine (just south of the mosque) has the best selection at the best prices.

The pottery's colouring comes from the touch of copper added to the glaze, and each piece is unique, crafted by a handful of Tamegroute families that have been working the pottery kilns for centuries. Covetable items include bowls, plates and candlestick holders.

Souq Haggling Tips

o Exchange pleasantries first – don't even think about kicking off negotiations without saying hello and asking how the shopkeeper is.

o Work out what you'd be willing to pay for something before you ask the price. The initial price the vendor quotes may be based on how wealthy they perceive you to be, and nothing to do with the item's actual value.

o Counter with an offer that's about one-third of your max limit and negotiate from there.

o Accept mint tea if it's offered.

homeware, this treasure-filled shop will have you reviewing your baggage allowance. Fortunately there's a rooftop cafe where you can make a decision over a glass of mint tea. (36-mouassine-concept-store.business.site)

L'Art du Bain Savonnerie Artisanale   COSMETICS

28 🔒 MAP P64, G5

Art du Bain's biodegradable, pure olive-oil soaps carry the scent of Marrakesh in them: honey, orange blossom, jasmine, eucalyptus – there's even a chamomile milk version for children – plus scrubs and *ghassoul* clay for the hammam. Soaps come packaged in recycled paper with a contemporary mono-tone geometric design. The Hand of Fatima soap dishes make great souvenirs. (📞0666572707)

Souq Cherifia   DESIGN

29 🔒 MAP P64, E3

Short-circuit souq fatigue and head straight for this converted *funduq* (inn once used by caravans) where younger local designers congregate on the 1st floor in the Carré Créateurs (Artisan Sq). Pick up hand-embroidered hessian accessories from **Khmissa**, snazzy Berber-design *babouches* with chunky soles from **Tilila**, and top-quality argan oil, *amlou* (argan-nut butter) and beauty products from **Arganino**.

Souq Haddadine   ARTS & CRAFTS

30 🔒 MAP P64, G3

The blacksmith's souq is full of busy workshops where the sound of the metalworkers' hammers rings out. If you've been tempted by some of those lovely Moroccan lamps for sale throughout the souqs, buying direct here will probably get you the best price. It's difficult to find: follow the noise. (Blacksmith's Souq)

Sarah Maj   FASHION & ACCESSORIES

31 🔒 MAP P64, E1

Sarah Maj herself can often be found minding her medina boutique (she also has a store in Gueliz). The Moroccan–Italian designer has a contemporary style that mixes Italian materials with Moroccan design – her long shirt-dresses are particularly lovely. (https://sarahmaj.shop/)

Bibi Art
ARTS & CRAFTS

32 🔒 MAP P64, D5

Rabii and Abdel buy their own wool and work with 160 to 170 women in the High Atlas, Middle Atlas and lesser Atlas Mountains to produce quality carpets for their three-floor store in the Marrakesh medina. This is a hassle-free, carefully laid-out haven where shoppers can browse dozens of different techniques and styles, all beautifully handcrafted using traditional looms and stitching. (https://bibiartmoroccanrugs.com/)

Shtatto
CONCEPT STORE

33 🔒 MAP P64, H5

Shtatto groups some of the trendiest contemporary brands in Marrakesh in one spot: Hassan Hajjaj's iconic pop-art photography and accessories, stylist Amine Bendriouich's couture collection, Amir Laftimi's London-inspired hipster barbershop Nature Marrakech, and Nasire's sublime fine leather goods. Wind your way up to the Med-riffing rooftop cafe, where fashionable, well-manicured travellers hang out with juice, coffee and tajines. Find it on Instagram @shtattomarrakech. (📞0524375538)

Souq Haddadine

Soufiane Zarib

DESIGN

34 🔒 MAP P64, G5

A tiny branch of this superb carpet and homewares shop has popped up in Rabha Kedima. It's just big enough for a range of cushions and some beautifully crafted clothes. The main branch is in Rue Riad Laârous. Find it on Instagram @soufiane-zarib. (soufiane-zarib.com)

Assouss Cooperative d'Argane

COSMETICS

35 🔒 MAP P64, D4

This is the Marrakesh outlet of a women's organic-certified argan cooperative outside Essaouira. The all-female staff will ply you with free samples of *amlou* and proudly explain how their ultra-emollient prickly pear oil and gourmet dipping oils are made. You'll find it near Mouassine Fountain. (📞0524380125)

Apothicaire Tuareg

FOOD

36 🔒 MAP P64, G5

Serious foodies, you have found spice nirvana. Proprietor Abdel is happy to take shoppers through a spice 101. His old-fashioned shop is crammed to the rafters with day-to-day cooking spices, argan oil and the natural remedies that Moroccans use to cure illnesses and scare away mischievous *jinn*. You can get legit Taliouine saffron here for Dh60 per gram.

Saffron for sale

DANA McMAHAN/GETTY IMAGES ©

Shopping for Saffron

Saffron – the gold dust of the foodie world – is for sale throughout Marrakesh's souqs. But hold on to your cooking aprons, gourmet travellers: not all of it is exactly what it seems. That really cheap saffron that spice stalls are hawking for Dh10 to Dh20 per gram? That's usually safflower.

Real saffron (the stigmas of the saffron crocus) have a more delicate thread, are less garishly red than safflower and have a tiny yellow tip. It's expensive because the flowers are only harvested one month of the year, in October, and an acre only yields about 1.5kg: you need 100,000 threads for 1kg of saffron. The real stuff comes from the Moroccan town of Taliouine, and it costs about Dh60 per gram. Good places to buy it include Apothicaire Tuareg, Yannass (p57) and the Mellah Market.

Norya Ayron FASHION & ACCESSORIES
37 🔒 MAP P64, F2

Located in Le Jardin (p70), Algerian designer Norya Ayron's bijou boutique counts American actresses Maggie Gyllenhaal and Sharon Stone among its fans thanks to her contemporary take on traditional caftans and *abayas* (full-length robe-like dresses) in often fabulously loud silk prints. Velvety soft suede and leather bags, kitsch clutches and a select range of jewellery mean you can deck yourself out in complete boho-bling. (norya-ayron.com)

Herboristerie La Sagesse COSMETICS
38 🔒 MAP P64, G2

This tourist-friendly *herboristerie* selling all manner of Moroccan spices, herbal medicines and natural beauty treatments is a fifth-generation family business – ask Haj Brahim or his daughters to whizz you through the health properties of their bottled plant extracts. Herbalist businesses are 10-a-penny in the souqs, but this one is special for its roof terrace with an excellent view into the Almoravid Koubba (p87). (📞0524391160)

Explore 🧭

Kâat Ben Nahid & Bab Debbagh

Along with Mouassine, Kâat Ben Nahid is the core of the old medina, with scrawls of close-knit alleyways hiding 17th-century riads. On its western edge is the recently restored Ben Youssef Medersa and the Mnebhi Palace, now the Musée de Marrakech — one of many neighbourhood museums. To the east is Bab Debbagh and the city's malodorous tanneries.

The Short List

○ **Ben Youssef Medersa (p82)** *Imagining hundreds of students living in this magnificently restored theological college.*

○ **Maison de la Photographie (p84)** *Stepping back in time amid this fascinating collection of vintage photography.*

○ **Orientalist Museum (p87)** *Finding Jacques Majorelle and Salvador Dalí on display at this excellent riad painters gallery.*

○ **Le Foundouk (p89)** *Savouring Moroccan dishes while sipping cocktails at this rooftop restaurant.*

○ **Bab Debbagh Tanneries (p88)** *Following your nose to find Marrakesh's smelliest trade.*

Getting There & Around

🚶 Head due north through the Central Souqs and eventually you will stumble out at Place Ben Youssef. At night, the Rue Mouassine route is safer.

🚗 Ask for Place du Moukef if you need access to Kâat Ben Nahid by car.

Neighbourhood Map on p86

Musée de Marrakech (p87) ANA DEL CASTILLO/SHUTTERSTOCK ©

Top Experience

Gawp at the Superb Ben Youssef Medersa

The Merinids, known for their dedication to the arts, were the first to build a medersa (theological college) here in the 14th century. This most sublime example of historic Moroccan architecture was rebuilt in 1565 by the Saadian Sultan Abdallah Al Ghalib. It was the largest – and most important – medersa in Morocco, only closing its doors in 1960.

◎ MAP P86, C1

Courtyard

Emerging from the relative darkness of the entry hall through *mashrabiya* (latticed) doors, it's difficult to suppress a gasp of astonishment at the serene beauty of the courtyard (pictured). At 15m x 20m, the expanse is a relief after the tiny streets of the medina outside. A large pool is set in the marble floor, surrounded by channels that keep the water flowing. The water for this central pool and the hammam is kept moving by pipes at different levels. Note that the CGI movie at Le Jardin Secret in Mouassine explains this ancient hydraulic system further.

Decoration

The Arabic inscription over the entryway reads 'You who enter my door, may your highest hopes be exceeded'.

In the courtyard, the walls and columns are covered in *zellige* (colourful geometric mosaic tilework), with friezes of calligraphy above, then intricate stucco carving – look out for the Saadian-era pine cones and palms. All of this is topped by carved cedar wood. The honeycomb *muqarnas* (decorative plaster vaulting) on the domed ceiling in the prayer room opposite the entrance is particularly beautiful and the *mihrab* (prayer niche denoting the direction of Mecca) has finely sculpted marble.

Students' Lodgings

With 130 rooms, the *medersa* accommodated up to 800 students in dorms arranged on different levels around the main courtyard and around six smaller courtyards open to the sky to provide light. The ablutions room on the ground floor has four marble columns and a domed ceiling over a central water basin and surrounding latrine rooms (today transformed into modern toilets for visitors).

Top Experience 📷

Discover old Marrakesh at Maison de la Photographie

When Parisian Patrick Menac'h and Marrakshi Hamid Mergani realised they were both collecting vintage Moroccan photography, they decided to open a gallery to show their collections and so Maison de la Photographie was born. The result is a fascinating display of the lifestyles and landscapes that the first intrepid photographers in Morocco captured through their lenses.

🎯 MAP P86, E1

maisondelaphotographie.ma

Vintage Portraiture

Some exhibits change every six to 12 months, but the ground-floor courtyard and rooms fanning off it are usually devoted to portraiture. The subjects are diverse, from tribal tattooed women of the mountains to aristocratic Arab city dwellers from Fez. The stand-out image of the permanent collection is a mesmerising photo of Hamidou Laambre, a sub-Saharan servant, taken in 1885 by Arévalo, a librarian from Tangier.

Morocco's Photography Debut

The ground floor's back salon holds the gallery's oldest photos, showing the debut of photography in Morocco when the first Europeans arrived with cameras and began documenting life here. The exhibit includes images of Tangier taken between 1870 and 1900.

Landscapes & Lifestyles

The 1st floor chambers surrounding the balcony host large portfolios of engaging works by two mid-20th-century Europeans in particular: Hungarian Nicolas Muller (1940s) and Belgian Charles Henneghien (1960s). Don't miss the 1920s photos of the Saadian Tombs, Ben Youssef Mosque, Djemaa El Fna and Marrakesh's ramparts, with only empty desert stretching beyond.

High Atlas Life

As you climb the stairs to the rooftop terrace, pop into the small room where French photographer Daniel Chicault's High Atlas documentary is played. Filmed in 1956, the film is a fascinating view into rural life during that period and was the first colour documentary made in Morocco. Don't miss the autochromes dark room on this floor, displaying the only colour photographs in the gallery.

★ Top Tips

o Useful information cards (in several languages) are kept in wall folders throughout the gallery, aiding understanding of the images and the history of photography in Morocco.

o A small shop at the entry sells editioned prints from the original negatives of many of the works displayed in the gallery.

✕ Take a Break

o The Maison de la Photographie's own rooftop cafe (p91) is one of the highest viewing points in the medina and perfect for a coffee or mint tea.

o Just down the street, Le Trou Au Mur (p89) is a contemporary Moroccan restaurant that also serves international comfort food with panache – a wonderful spot for lunch with wine.

Kâat Ben Nahid & Bab Debbagh Maison de la Photographie

Kâat Ben Nahid & Bab Debbagh

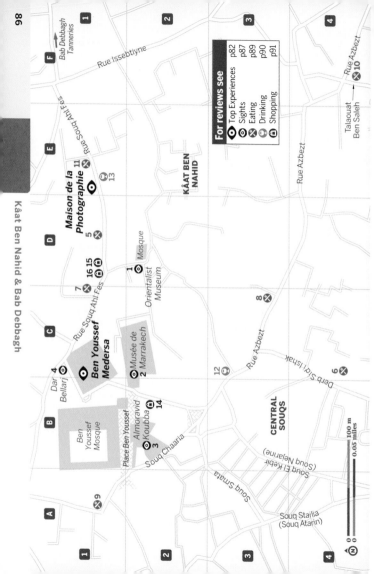

Bab Debbagh Tanneries

Rue Issebtiyne

F
1
2
3
4

Rue Souq Ahl Fes

Maison de la Photographie 11 ⊗

E
⊙ 13

KÂAT BEN NAHID

Rue Azbezt

Talaouat Ben Saleh

Rue Azbezt
⊗ 10

For reviews see
⊙ Top Experiences	p82
⊙ Sights	p87
⊗ Eating	p89
⊙⊙ Drinking	p90
⊙ Shopping	p91

D
5 ⊗
16 15
⊙⊙
7 ⊗
⊙ Mosque
1 ⊙
Orientalist Museum

C
Rue Souq Ahl Fes
Dar ⊙ 4 Bellarj
Ben Youssef Medersa ⊙
Musée de ⊙ 2 Marrakech

8 ⊗

Rue Azbezt

Derb Sidi Ishak

Rue Azbezt

B
Ben Youssef Mosque
Place Ben Youssef
Almoravid ⊙ Koubba 14
⊙ 3
Souq Chaaria

12 ⊙

CENTRAL SOUQS

6 ⊗

A
⊗ 9

Souq Smata

Souq El Kebir (Souq Nejarine)

Souq Stailia (Souq Atarin)

100 m
0.05 miles

1
2
3
4

Sights

Orientalist Museum
MUSEUM

1 ⊙ MAP P86, D2

Opened as a sister museum to MACMA (p132) in Gueliz, this small private gallery beautifully displays the big guns of Orientalist painting inside a 17th-century riad. The impressive collection of 19th- and 20th-century European artists who fell for Morocco's landscapes and peoples include Eugène Delacroix, Henri Le Riche, Edy Legrand and, of course, Jacques Majorelle – he of garden fame. There's even a Salvador Dalí in here. Complete your tour with a coffee in the tranquil rooftop **cafe**. (https://theorientalistmuseumof marrakech.business.site)

Musée de Marrakech
MUSEUM

2 ⊙ MAP P86, C2

The Musée de Marrakech exhibits a collection of Moroccan art forms within the decadent salons of the Mnebhi Palace. The central internal courtyard, with its riot of cedar archways, stained-glass windows, intricate painted door panels and, of course, lashings of *zellige* (colourful geometric mosaic tilework), is the highlight, though don't miss the display of exquisite Fez ceramics in the main room off the courtyard, and the palace's hammam. This is one of Marrakesh's oldest museums and looks dated compared with some others. (☎0524441893)

Almoravid Koubba
HISTORIC BUILDING

3 ⊙ MAP P86, B2

The Almohads destroyed almost everything their Almoravid predecessors built in Marrakesh but overlooked this graceful 12th-century *koubba* (shrine) across from the Ben Youssef Mosque. This relic reveals what Hispano-Moorish architecture owes to the Almoravids: keyhole arches, interlaced arabesques and a domed cupola on a crenellated base. It was probably the ablution block of the adjacent mosque, and if you climb down the steps, you can see the system of pipes that supplied it with water. The inside decoration is particularly fine.

Almoravid Koubba

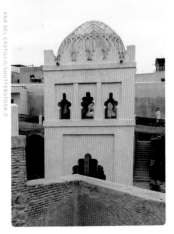

ANA DEL CASTILLO/SHUTTERSTOCK ©

Kâat Ben Nahid & Bab Debbagh Sights

Bab Debbagh
Tanneries

Leather working is one of Morocco's medieval trades, and the **tanneries** (Association Sidi Yacoub; Map p86) around Bab Debbagh – ideally situated next to the river from where they draw water to pummel animal hides – have been in use for hundreds of years. The largest cooperative, Association Sidi Yacoub, is down a lane just inside the gate, on the southern side of Rue de Bab Debbagh – you'll know you've reached it when the acrid smell assaults your nose.

The pungent smell comes from the use of ammonia in the troughs that's used to soften the leather and strip it of its animal hairs. Unlike the tanneries in Fez, you won't see a rainbow of dyes used; here the tanneries only work the natural leather, and dyeing is done elsewhere. Surrounding the roughly hewn troughs of clay, you'll find the leatherworkers' workshops, which have been handed down from generation to generation. It's hard, dirty work and exclusively a male industry.

Beware the Scams: Tips for Visiting

◦ The Association Sidi Yacoub's signboard declares the tanneries are open to visitors and free to visit, but it's likely you'll be accosted by a 'guardian' at the entrance telling you otherwise. Insist upon entering without a 'guide', which will cost you dearly. Fob them off with a small tip of Dh10 to Dh20 only if you have to.

◦ If you're not up for this battle, go with an official guide as part of a medina tour; this is the only way to ensure you skip the hassle.

◦ The best time to come is in the morning when you'll usually be able to see tanners at work, transforming stinking animal skins dropped off by donkey carts.

◦ The bird's-eye views from the houses surrounding the tanneries offer a completely different perspective, but be aware that many are actually leatherware shops, and touts can be pushy. Give a tip of Dh10 to Dh20 for access, and don't feel pressured to buy.

◦ Beware the young men on foot or motorbikes who will follow you from the central souqs and then may insist upon entering with you for an extortionate fee. To avoid this, we recommend getting a taxi to the outside of Bab Debbagh and walking into the medina, as the tanneries are just inside the gate.

Dar Bellarj

GALLERY

4 💿 MAP P86, C1

Flights of fancy come with the territory at Dar Bellarj, a stork hospital (*bellarj* is Arabic for stork) turned into Marrakesh's premier arts centre. Each year the nonprofit Dar Bellarj Foundation adopts a programme themed around living culture, ranging from film to women's textiles and storytelling. Admission is usually free (there's a charge for some events). Exhibitions are usually in French and Arabic. (📞0524444555)

Eating

Le Foundouk

MOROCCAN $$$

5 🍴 MAP P86, D1

A spidery iron chandelier lit with candles sets the mood for fine dining, with Moroccan and international menus. Portions aren't huge, but great care is taken to present dishes beyond the run-of-the-mill tourist options, such as confit leg of lamb with garlic, saffron and quince, and seven-cereal couscous with fish, broccoli and artichokes. Booking online is recommended. (www.foundouk.com; 📶)

L'Mida

MOROCCAN $$

6 🍴 MAP P86, C4

Push open the studded door and climb up to the pretty green, white and mustard decor on the 1st floor and rooftop. The excellent modern Moroccan fare is curated by executive chef and cookbook author Narjisse Benkabbou. You can expect Berber gnocchi or sea bream poke bowl with a sweet-and-sour chermoula sauce. There's a children's menu too. No alcohol. (https://lmidamarrakech.com)

Le Trou Au Mur

MEDITERRANEAN $$$

7 🍴 MAP P86, C1

The menu at this classy yet laid-back contemporary restaurant is on the money with its mix of little-seen Moroccan dishes, fusion food and international crowd pleasers. Stay cool in the mod dining room or head to the rooftop for giant martinis, Berber shepherd's pie, mac and cheese or the house speciality of *mechoui* (slow-roasted lamb). (letrouaumur.com; ❄️📶)

Naima

MOROCCAN $$

8 🍴 MAP P86, C3

If you want to eat couscous prepared by a proper Marrakshi mama, then Naima is the place to be. Squeeze into the tiny dining room, let the chef serve you her daily feast of chicken and vegetable couscous (there's no menu, and little English is spoken) – and settle back with the local radio and a mint tea as the women get cooking.

Chez Rachid

MOROCCAN $

9 🍴 MAP P86, A1

Firing up the grill from his cubby-hole kitchen, young Rachid dishes up hearty, simple meals of grilled brochettes (kebabs), cutlets and *merguez* (spicy sausage) that come with olives, *harissa* (hot chilli paste), tomato salad and lentils. Tables spread across the wide alleyway, making this an interesting spot for a cheap and tasty lunch.

Roti d'Or INTERNATIONAL $

10 MAP P86, F4

Blink and you'd miss it, but Roti d'Or is not a place to walk by if you're looking for a good-value alternative to Moroccan food. The theme is Tex-Mex and, though it's not very authentic, it's plenty tasty. Menu options like Tex-Mex burgers and falafel wraps all come with fries and olives; the spiced chicken burrito is a bargain. (📞0675452260; 📶✏)

Dar Tazi MOROCCAN $

11 MAP P86, E1

We like the smiley staff here. The restaurant itself has old-fashioned, homey appeal, a roof terrace and a dependable menu of *briouats* (fried savoury stuffed pastries), *bastilla* (savoury-sweet pie) and Berber chicken tajine. Its location next to the Maison de la Photographie makes it a good lunch stop, or snack on Moroccan pastries and mint tea for Dh40. (📞0524378382)

Drinking

Kafe Merstan CAFE

12 MAP P86, C3

Right in the centre of the medina souqs, Merstan's roof terrace is a great place to escape for a fresh

Mint tea

MARCQ MAYER/SHUTTERSTOCK ©

juice or a mint or cinnamon tea. Friendly service, good views and comfy shaded seating cloaked in traditional *boucharouite* rugs make this the perfect spot to refresh and recharge. (kafemerstan.ma; 📶)

Maison de la Photographie Terrace CAFE

13 🎧 MAP P86, E1

This panoramic terrace is one of the highest in the medina, and it's a wonderful place to sit back and admire the terracotta rooftops with a fruit juice or mint tea after visiting the photography gallery (p84) downstairs. (maisondela photographie.ma)

Shopping

La Qoubba Galerie d'Art ART

14 🔒 MAP P86, B2

This smart yet approachable gallery knocks the socks off the medina art shops and stalls. It's a showroom for well-regarded contemporary Moroccan artists, the quality is noticeably higher than elsewhere, and artworks come with certificates of authenticity. Gallery manager Mohammed has a wealth of knowledge about the artists and can arrange shipping. (www.qoubbagalerie.com)

Fibre Trip TEXTILES

15 🔒 MAP P86, D1

You can watch beautiful quality wool and linen scarves being wo-

Don't Leave Morocco Without... 🛍️

Moroccan teapot Moroccan mint tea is known for its refreshing aromas of fresh spearmint and sweet notes of green tea. Prepare it at home in a traditional Moroccan tea pot.

Cosmetic argan oil Argan oil is globally renowned for its cosmetic virtues – did you know that Morocco is the sole producer of argan oil in the world?

Almond pastries Morocco is known for its countless types of pastries made with almond paste and flavoured with orange-blossom water or rosewater. Look for gazelle horns and honey *briouats*.

Recommended by Nargisse Benkabbou, *executive chef at L'Mida (p89) restaurant and author of cookbook* Casablanca: My Moroccan Food. @mymoroccanfood

ven by hand here on a traditional loom. (📞 0642223758)

Bennoun Faissal TEXTILES

16 🔒 MAP P86, D1

This friendly store sells fixed-price hand-loomed cotton, wool, silk and linen scarves of exceptional quality.

Explore ⊕

Kasbah & Mellah

When the Almoravids founded Marrakesh in 1062, the Kasbah area was where they set up camp. Kasbahs (fortresses) were erected for the glory and protection of warmongering sultans. Many of Morocco's top historical sites lie in this area of the medina, but tour groups rarely linger and the atmosphere is quite mellow. Adjoining the Kasbah is the Mellah – Marrakesh's old Jewish quarter.

The Short List

○ **Bahia Palace (p94)** *Craning your neck at ceiling splendour in a succession of unparalleled regal salons at one of Marrakesh's biggest historic sights.*

○ **Saadian Tombs (p96)** *Paying homage at Sultan Al Mansour's mausoleum, an all-in blowout of marble.*

○ **Lazama Synagogue (p101)** *Learning about the history of Jews in Marrakesh at one of the Mellah's few still-functioning synagogues.*

○ **Cafe Clock (p103)** *Tapping into local culture at this cafe where traditional hikayat (storytelling) is being revived and Marrakshi musicians regularly play.*

○ **Badi Palace (p101)** *Viewing storks nests from the ramparts of this 16th-century ruin.*

Getting There & Around

🚶 It's a 10-minute walk from Djemaa El Fna to Place des Ferblantiers down Rue Riad Zitoun El Jedid or Rue Riad Zitoun El Kedim.

🚗 Ask for Palais de la Bahia or Place des Ferblantiers.

Calèche For a scenic option, hire a horse-drawn carriage from the stand just off Djemaa El Fna.

Neighbourhood Map on p100

Badi Palace (p101) NICK KEE SON/GETTY IMAGES ©

Top Experience 📷

Take in the Grandeur of Bahia Palace

Imagine the pomp and splendour you'd dream up with Morocco's top artisans at your beck and call, and here you have it. La Bahia (The Beautiful) is an 8000-sq-metre floor-to-ceiling extravagance of intricate marquetry, plasterwork and zouak (painted wood), begun by Grand Vizier Si Moussa in the 1860s but expanded by his son and successor Abu 'Bou' Ahmed.

◉ MAP P100, C1
📞 0524389564

Petit Riad

Closest to the entrance, the single-storey Petit Riad has walls of intensely elaborate white plasterwork, inscribed with verses from the Quran. In the 19th century when it was originally decorated, this plaster would have been carved in situ while wet – just imagine the artisan skill required to work so swiftly and accurately.

This area of the palace was a later addition, built in Bou Ahmed's era and where he would have received government officials. After Morocco became a French protectorate in 1912, the Petit Riad was used as the private apartments of the French Resident-General in Marrakesh, who added electricity and heating.

Cour d'Honneur

Sandwiched between the Petit Riad and the Grand Riad, the Grand Cour, or Cour d'Honneur (pictured), is the undisputed heart of the palace – a spectacular open space of 1500 sq metres, restored to its original brilliance in 2018. The floor is a vast expanse of Italian Carrara marble, encircled by a gallery uniquely coloured with bright blue and yellow plaster and woodwork. When Bou Ahmed became Grand Vizier in 1894 and expanded the palace, this section was converted into a harem for his four wives and 24 concubines.

Grand Riad

Step through the doorway from the Cour d'Honneur into the lush fountain courtyard of the Grand Riad. This is the oldest part of the palace complex, completed in 1867 by Si Moussa, a former slave who rose through the ranks to become one of Sultan Hassan I's most important aides. The riad's salon is bedecked with carved wood lintels, *zouak* artistry and stained-glass detailing – Bahia Palace was thought to be the first building in North Africa to use stained glass as a decorative feature.

★ **Top Tips**

o Tour groups descend throughout the day, so come for opening or late afternoon if you can.

o Leave plenty of time to admire the site, so that you can pause and wait for passing groups to dissipate – large tours can overrun whole rooms.

o The palm-shaded entry garden is a great place to stop for a minute and get your map bearings before heading back onto the street.

✕ **Take a Break**

o Head up Rue Riad Zitoun El Jdid to Mandala Society (p50) for one of its speciality coffees or teas.

o For an afternoon drink with a view, skip across the road to Kosybar (p105) in Place des Ferblantiers.

Top Experience 📷
Explore the Saadian Tombs

Sultan Al Mansour was just as extravagant in death as he was in life. After the 'golden king' built Badi Palace in the 16th century, he transformed an existing necropolis into this lavish tomb complex. He certainly wasn't counting on Alaouite Sultan Moulay Ismail walling it up a few decades later. The mausoleum lay forgotten until aerial photography exposed it in 1917.

◉ MAP P100, B2

Chamber of 12 Pillars

The tomb complex's main chamber (pictured) is to the left of the site entrance – just look for the queue. At the time of writing, it could only be admired through an arched viewing door, though plans are afoot to build a viewing platform circling the chamber to help ease congestion. Elaborate *zellige* (colourful geometric mosaic tilework) and gilded honeycomb *muqarnas* (decorative plaster vaulting) abound in this hall, which gets its name from the fact that its cupola ceiling is supported by three groups of four pillars of Italian Carrara marble. Two of these columns are noticeably older – plundered loot from the ancient Roman city of Volubilis.

Chamber of Three Niches & Prayer Room

Surrounding the central Chamber of 12 Pillars are two other tomb rooms. Alpha princes were buried in the Chamber of the Three Niches, while the room to the left was originally a prayer room. The intricately carved, pentagon-shaped feature in the back wall is the *mihrab* (prayer niche).

Lalla Massouda's Tomb

The cemetery's secondary mausoleum was erected in 1557 and predates the rest of the complex. Al Mansour claimed it for his mother, Lalla Massouda. Hers is the singular tomb recessed in a niche at the back of the mausoleum; the rest belong to other important women of the court.

Next to this structure you can still see the original main entrance to the tombs, blocked up by Moulay Ismail and never reopened. Accessible for centuries only through a small passage in the Moulay El Yazid Mosque, the tombs were neglected by all except the storks until the French discovered them and built the alleyway in the southwestern corner through which visitors now enter.

★ **Top Tips**

○ The site is busy with tour groups from about 9.30am to 1pm, and a long queue can form to view Al Mansour's chamber.

○ Late afternoon is the best time for photography as the marble work takes on a golden hue in the light.

○ The entrance is not easy to spot. Walk to the southern end of the Moulay El Yazid Mosque, with the Kasbah Café directly across the road, and head through the archway.

✗ **Take a Break**

○ Across the road from the Saadian Tombs entrance, Kasbah Café (p105) is a top spot to recharge.

○ For camel burgers, date milkshakes and a fun vibe, head down Rue de la Kasbah to Cafe Clock (p103).

Cycling Tour 🚲

A Royal Loop Around Kasbah

The sprawling southern Kasbah quarter and its mellow local streets are perfect for two-wheeled exploration. Use Marrakesh's bike-sharing scheme, starting at the Medina Bike (p147) kiosk in front of Koutoubia Mosque.

Cycle Facts

Start & End Koutoubia Mosque

Length 5km; one to two hours

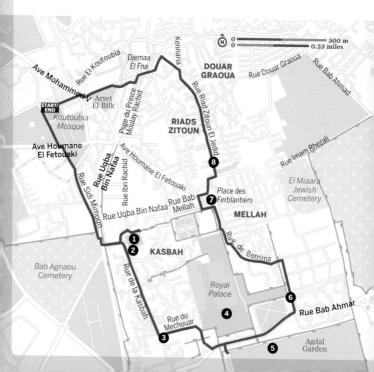

❶ Moulay El Yazid Mosque

Circle behind the **Koutoubia Mosque** (p42) to head south on Rue Sidi Mimoun, turning left and then right through two fortification archways, onto Rue de la Kasbah. The giant Moulay El Yazid Mosque on your left was built in 1190. At dusk, neighbourhood women come out to gossip on its pedestrianised plaza.

❷ Saadian Tombs

Keep going south down Rue de la Kasbah past the **Saadian Tombs** (p96). After the road narrows, local street life takes over. Smoke wafts out of grill stalls and grease-covered mechanics fix motorbikes at hole-in-the-wall garages.

❸ Cafe Clock

At the point where you need to turn left, you'll find **Cafe Clock** (p103) on the corner. This cafe is a hub for young, creative Marrakshis – its entrance is usually surrounded by excellent street art.

❹ Royal Palace

Heading east, the next widening of the road is the best spot to pause for a glimpse of the Royal Palace. It's closed to the public, but its red crenellated walls dominate the ride from here on – by royal decree, no buildings in this part of the medina are allowed to rise above two storeys in case they should overlook the palace.

❺ Agdal Garden

If the royal **Agdal Garden** (p103) is open, extend your trip south. A gravel path cuts through orange, date, lemon, fig, walnut and pomegranate trees to a pavilion and broad pool. You can pay the guardians Dh10 or so to mind your bike.

❻ Rue de Berrima

Skirt around the southern and eastern walls of the palace, cutting back into the Mellah (Jewish quarter) to join untouristy Rue de Berrima northbound, catching a pungent whiff of sardines being bartered over at produce stalls.

❼ Place des Ferblantiers

Eventually, the terracotta-red walls of the Royal Palace will morph into the stork-inhabited ones of the 16th-century **Badi Palace** (p101). Head through the arched entrance to **Place des Ferblantiers**, once an ancient metalworking hub.

❽ Riad Zitoun El Jedid

Finish your ride northbound through the medina artery of Riad Zitoun El Jedid and across **Djemaa El Fna** (p38) if you dare, or take the busy main road up Ave Houmane El Fetouaki back to the Koutoubia Mosque.

Kasbah & Mellah

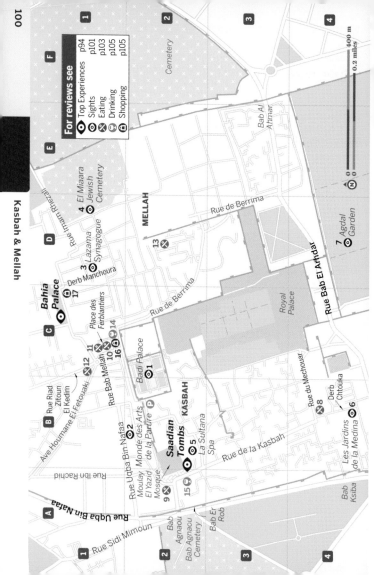

For reviews see	
◉ Top Experiences	p94
◎ Sights	p101
⊗ Eating	p103
⊗ Drinking	p105
⋒ Shopping	p105

Cemetery

El Miaara
4 ◎ Jewish
Cemetery

3 ◎ Lazama
Synagogue

Derb Manchoura

Bahia
Palace

Place des
Ferblantiers

Rue Riad
Zitoun
El Kedim

Ave Houmane El Fetouaki

Rue Bab Mellah

Rue Iman Rifa'izali

MELLAH

Rue de Berrima

13 ⊗

Rue de Berrima

Rue de Berrima

Badi
Palace

1 ◎

Royal
Palace

Rue Bab El Arhdar

7 ◎ Agdal
Garden

Bab Al
Ahmar

Rue Uqba Bin Nafaa

Moulay
El Yazid
Mosque

Monde des Arts
de la Parure

2 ◎

Saadian
Tombs

5 ◎

KASBAH

La Suitana
Spa

Rue du Mechouar

Derb
Chtouka

8 ⊗

6 ◎ Les Jardins
de la Medina

Rue de la Kasbah

Rue Ibn Rachid

9 ⊗

15 ⋒

Bab
Agnaou

Bab Agnaou
Cemetery

Bab Er
Rob

Bab
Ksiba

Rue Sidi Mimoun

Rue Uqba Bin Nafaa

12 ⊗
11 ⊗
10 ⊗ 14
16 ⋒

17 ⋒

0   400 m
0   0.2 miles

Sights

Badi Palace
HISTORIC SITE

1 ◉ MAP P100, C2

As 16th-century Sultan Ahmed Al Mansour (r 1578–1603) was paving the Badi Palace with gold, turquoise and crystal, his court jester wisecracked, 'It'll make a beautiful ruin'. That jester was no fool: at the beginning of the 18th century, the place was destroyed by Sultan Moulay Ismail and materials carried off to then-capital Meknes. Today only remnants remain, watched over by nesting storks. There are magnificent views from the ramparts.

Monde des Arts de la Parure
MUSEUM

2 ◉ MAP P100, B2

Step over the moat into this impressive museum and prepare to be awestruck by the superb displays of jewellery, saddlery, adornments, textiles and ceremonial garments from around the world. Nearly 3000 pieces from more than 50 countries are professionally curated, expertly lit and, in a first for a Moroccan museum, each display carries a QR code to scan so that all is explained in English and French on your phone. There's a rooftop restaurant, as well as a gift and book shop. Tickets can be booked online. Guided tours are available. (MAP Marrakech; https://lemapmarrakech.com)

Koutoubia's Prayer Pulpit

A highlight of the Badi Palace is the room housing the intricate Koutoubia minbar (prayer pulpit). If you're curious about the craftsmanship within Marrakesh's mosques but can't see inside them, be sure to pay it a visit. Once inside the Koutoubia Mosque, the minbar's cedarwood steps with gold and silver calligraphy were the work of 12th-century Cordoban artisans headed by a man named Aziz.

Lazama Synagogue
SYNAGOGUE

3 ◉ MAP P100, D1

Only a couple of synagogues in the Mellah are still used by Marrakesh's dwindling Jewish community, including this one, which doubles as an interesting museum of Jewish life in Morocco. It was originally built in 1492 by Jews expelled from Spain, but its blue-and-white interior is a much later iteration. The synagogue is on the right-hand side of the pretty internal courtyard – note the Star of David motif in *zellige* (colourful geometric mosaic tilework). (Slat Al Azama; jmarrakech.org)

El Miaara Jewish Cemetery
CEMETERY

4 ◉ MAP P100, D1

Burial grounds in Morocco are typically closed to non-Muslim visitors, but this sprawling walled Jewish cemetery of whitewashed tombs admits all who wish to pay their respects. It dates from the 12th century and is still in use. It's well maintained by Marrakesh's small Jewish community – you'll see rocks of remembrance on top of some of the tombs. (jmarrakech.org)

La Sultana Spa SPA

5 ◉ MAP P100, B2

La Sultana's opulent spa is one of the most luxurious and profes- sional in the medina. Signature body scrubs and facial treatments use spices plus argan and prickly- pear oils, and the spa also offers a high-end traditional hammam experience. The icing on the cake is the column-flanked indoor pool

room with Jacuzzi and fireplace, dripping with Moroccan lanterns. Book ahead. (lasultanamarrakech. com)

Les Jardins de la Medina SWIMMING

6 ◉ MAP P100, B4

This 19th-century palace-turned- boutique hotel and bar is the most beautiful place in the southern medina for a light lunch and afternoon lounging poolside. The huge riad garden is planted with old palms, orange and olive trees, and jacarandas that burst into dramatic blue bloom in early sum- mer. The pool and lunch package available to nonguests includes a towel and lounger. Book ahead. (lesjardinsdelamedina.com)

Zeitoun Cafe

Agdal Garden

GARDENS

7 ⊙ MAP P100, D4

Built in the 12th century by the founder of the Almohad caliphate, Agdal was once the most important garden in Marrakesh. Although the gardens and its pools cover a huge expanse along the southern edges of the walled medina, only a fraction of it is accessible to the public because Agdal backs onto the Royal Palace. From the Saadian Tombs it's about a 45-minute walk south – consider renting a bike to get down here.

Eating

Cafe Clock

CAFE $$

8 ✗ MAP P100, B4

Little sister to the Fez original, Cafe Clock is housed in an old school with sunset views over the Kasbah from its rooftop. The food, including veggie options like the falafel super bowl and vegetable *bastilla* (savoury-sweet pie), is decent – tourists delight in the signature camel burger. However, its popularity rests on its packed calendar of cultural performances, which also attracts many young Marrakshis. (cafeclock.com; 🛜 ✎ 🖆)

Zeitoun Cafe

MOROCCAN $$

9 ✗ MAP P100, A2

Tajine options don't vary much among restaurants in Marrakesh, but Zeitoun Cafe offers up lesser-known options, such as *tajine makfoul* with beef, tomato

and onion chutney and grilled almonds, fish tajine with saffron and olives or its signature camel *tanjia* (slow-cooked stew). Service can be a bit slow, but if you snag a seat on a cosy banquette overlooking the Moulay El Yazid Mosque, who's clock-watching? (zeitouncafe. com; 🛜 👬)

Chez Kamal & Brahim

MOROCCAN $

10 ✗ MAP P100, C1

The plastic tables and chairs fronting Place des Ferblantiers make this restaurant look like a tourist trap, but through the back, it doubles as a busy grill stall for locals on a parallel street. The tourist menu is solid enough, but our money is on the grilled *kefta* (meatballs).

Mazel Streetfood Coffee

MEDITERRANEAN $$

11 ✗ MAP P100, C1

Sit down at the green *zellige* tables of Mazel Streetfood Coffee on pretty Place des Ferblantiers and try the pita and falafels, a vegetarian quinoa bowl or choose from the Moroccan menu. The speciality coffees are good. It's just the place for a rest under the shady umbrellas.

Dar Anika

MOROCCAN $$$

12 ✗ MAP P100, C1

Dar Anika is a luxury riad hotel, but its roof terrace, framed by palms and covered like a giant Berber tent, is all about formal candlelit dining set to live music. Opt for the

Medina
Architecture 101

The medina, the old walled part of the city, has its own distinctive urban layout and forms of architecture. The twisty labyrinth of alleyways will keep you wondering what's behind that wall or down that block. Here are some of the most common medina features you'll see.

Kasbahs

This extra-fortified quarter housed the ruling family and all the necessities for living in case of a siege. Marrakesh's 11th-century kasbah is one of the largest remaining in Morocco and still houses a royal palace.

Ramparts

The Almoravids wrapped Marrakesh in 19km of pink *pisé* (rammed earth) walls, 2m thick, punctuated by 19 *biban* (gates; singular *bab*). These dramatic and defensive walls still separate the medina from the Ville Nouvelle today.

Religious Buildings

Non-Muslims cannot enter any of the mosques in Marrakesh but are able to admire the striking minarets from outside. The square design is inherited from local Amazigh tradition, rather than being of Arab origin. Marrakesh also has seven *zawiyas* (shrines to a *marabout* – saint). You'll recognise these by their green ceramic-tiled roofs, often accompanied by a *koubba* (domed-roof structure).

Riads & Dars

So many riads have become hotels in recent years that the word has become a synonym for 'guesthouse', but technically an authentic riad has a courtyard garden divided in four parts, with a fountain in the centre. A *dar*, on the other hand, is also a traditional courtyard house, but one without a central garden.

Souqs & Qissariat

Souqs are the medina's market streets. They're crisscrossed with smaller streets lined with storerooms and cubby-hole-sized artisans' studios. Unlike souqs, these smaller streets often do not have names and are together known as a *qissaria*. Most *qissariat* are through-streets, so when (not if) you get lost in them, keep heading onward until you intersect with the next souq.

Moroccan dishes rather than the Italian ones; for a sweet-savoury kick, order the chicken *seffa medfouna*, which is topped with raisins, almonds and cinnamon-spiked vermicelli. (riaddaranika.com)

La Table Al Badia   MOROCCAN $$$

13 🍴 MAP P100, D2

This highly atmospheric French-run riad is a top choice for Moroccan cooking, with *dada* (chef) Samira at the helm serving up her own take on the country's classics. Produce is bought from the market each day, so everything's fresh: walk-ins cannot be accommodated. Book at least a day ahead, and try to get a table on the rooftop. (riadalbadia.com; 🖊)

Drinking

Kosybar   BAR

14 🍺 MAP P100, C1

Mid-afternoon this is the closest the medina gets to an actual bar. The Marrakesh-meets-Kyoto interiors are full of plush, private nooks, but keep heading upstairs to low-slung canvas sofas on the rooftop terrace where storks give beer drinkers the once-over from nearby nests. Skip the expensive meals and stick with the bar snacks. (kosybar.com; 📶)

Kasbah Café   CAFE

15 ☕ MAP P100, A2

Come sunset, the roof terrace of this cafe is a prime viewing platform for the unfurling nightly social life around the Kasbah's Moulay El Yazid Mosque. Relax with a fresh juice, milkshake or mint tea as locals come out to gossip and congregate below, and perhaps grab one of the giant pizzas if you can't peel yourself away. (kasbahcafemarrakech.com; 📶)

Les Jardins de la Medina   BAR

Mature palms and soothing fountains create a relaxing little enclave at this courtyard bar within a classy 1920s Kasbah hotel (see 6 ◎ Map p100, B4). Live musicians can often be found strumming and warbling while well-dressed guests take pre-dinner aperitifs in green wicker armchairs. (lesjardinsdela medina.com; 📶)

Shopping

Concept Bohem   HOMEWARES

16 🔒 MAP P100, C1

Tucked into the corner of the square, Concept Bohem is a great place to browse among the baskets galore, grass mats, crochet and macrame bags and plant hangers, blankets, light fittings and mirrors.

Atelier El Bahia   ARTS & CRAFTS

17 🔒 MAP P100, C1

For honest salespeople and good-quality local textiles, family-run Atelier El Bahia is a great choice. It's a proper emporium with fixed prices and made-to-measure service: look for the weavers working hand looms in the front window.

Explore ⊛

Bab Doukkala & Riad Laârous

Welcome to the medina's shrinking violets: quiet neighbourhoods with few visitor attractions and still enough local residents to outnumber tourists. But therein lies their charm. Bab Doukkala in particular is a wonderful window into Marrakshi life. Its name comes from the Doukkala tribe that centuries ago would have used this gate to enter Marrakesh on trade forays.

The Short List

∘ **La Maison Arabe (p114)** *Lapping up the luxurious setting of the granddaddy of medina restaurants, perhaps signing up for one of its quickie cooking classes.*

∘ **Henna Cafe (p114)** *Getting etched with a piece of temporary body art at this friendly cafe that funds education and community projects.*

∘ **Riad Kniza Musée & Galerie (p111)** *Learning about Amazigh sugar hammers and antique High Atlas carpets in Bab Doukkala's first museum.*

∘ **Two-wheeled adventures (p111)** *Cycling medina backstreets with community-minded Pikala Bikes.*

∘ **Mustapha Blaoui (p116)** *Unearthing a unique souvenir in this treasure-trove emporium.*

Getting There & Around

✈ Head north from Djemaa El Fna up Rue Fatima Zahra and Rue Dar El Glaoui.

🚌 No 1 from Djemaa El Fna to Place Bab Doukkala.

🚗 Car access is good: Rue Dar El Glaoui is a convenient taxi drop-off point.

Neighbourhood Map on p110

Walking Tour 🥾

Stroll Around Bab Doukkala

Had enough of sequinned babouches (leather slippers) and carpet sellers? Take a breather in the streets of mellow Bab Doukkala, where the only haggling that's being done is around old-fashioned neighbourhood stores, fragrant herb carts and glistening fish stalls. This is a real residential area, with friendly locals and unexpected arty credentials.

Walk Facts

Start Bab Doukkala gate
End Derb El Halfaoui
Length 1km; two hours

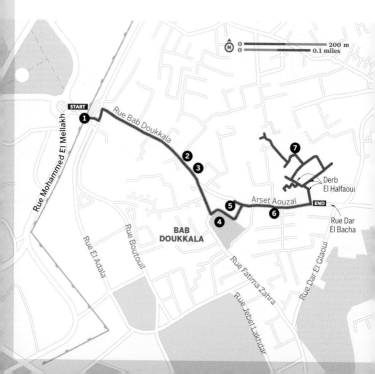

❶ Enter Through Bab Doukkala

In the 12th-century glory days, the hulking gate of Bab Doukkala is where caravanserais carrying the lowland Amazigh Doukkala tribe would have entered the city. The original gate, now closed off, is to the northeast. The double horse-shoe archway is a later addition built to accommodate road traffic.

❷ Souq Life

Stroll Bab Doukkala's lively local souq, where lamb haunches hang off butchers' hooks, farmers lay out blankets of walnuts, and local women come to assess the freshness of slippery sardines and earth-clod veg. Head south-east past the sizzling grills and eventually you'll pass the **public fountain** where locals pause to wash their hands before handling souq produce.

❸ Watch Pastry Makers

A little south of the fountain, look for the metal drum stoves where skilled pastry makers twirl *warqa* (filo-like pastry), which is sold in batches to create *bastilla* (a savoury-sweet pie layered with pigeon or chicken). Watch how they deftly pat the ball of dough onto the searing hot plate in a con-tinuous circular motion to create gossamer-thin pastry sheets.

❹ Mosque Activity

The **Bab Doukkala Mosque** sits beside a small square, its minaret towering above the palm trees. This local plaza is always a hive of activity and a hangout for horse-and-cart delivery folk catching a break in the shade.

❺ Doukkala Fountain

Swing by the furniture-maker workshops on the mosque's north side to arrive at the restored Douk-kala Fountain with its intricate lintel. The building adjoining it has been redeveloped as a cultural centre, but used to be a public swimming pool that, like the nearby **hammam** (p113), was fed by the fountain waters.

❻ Henna Cafe Break

Take a break at friendly **Henna Cafe** (p114). On the ground floor, you might spot where your money is going: look out for the packed classroom providing education for local residents.

❼ Derb Street Art

By far the most interesting *derb* (alleyway) in Bab Doukkala is Derb El Halfaoui. Almost immediately as you enter on your right, take a peek inside the wood-stoked local bakery piled with sacks of loaves. Further down, it becomes an amateur street-art gallery filled with scenes of Sahara dunes and kasbahs.

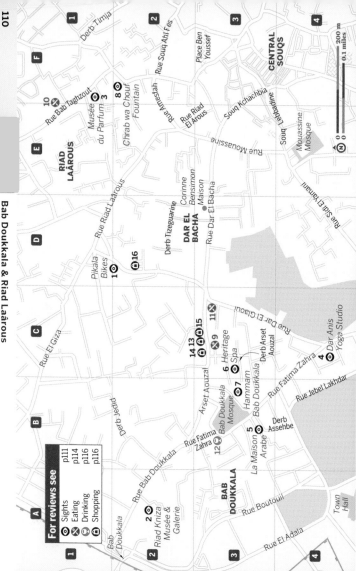

For reviews see

⊙	Sights	p111
⊗	Eating	p114
⊘	Drinking	p116
⊡	Shopping	p116

RIAD LAÂROUS

BAB DOUKKALA

DAR EL BACHA

CENTRAL SOUQS

Derb Timja

Rue Bab Taghzout

Rue Souq Ahl Fes

Place Ben Youssef

Musée du Parfum

Chrab wa Chouf Fountain

Rue Amesfah

Rue Riad El Arous

Souq Kchachbia

Souq 'Labbadine

Rue Moussine

Mouassine Mosque

Rue Sidi El Yamani

Rue Riad Laârous

Corinne Bensimon Maison

Derb Tizeguarine

Rue Dar El Bacha

Pikala Bikes

Rue El Giza

Derb Jedid

Rue Bab Doukkala

Arset Aouzal

Rue Dar El Giaoui

Heritage Spa

Derb Arset Aouzal

Dar Anis Yoga Studio

Rue Fatima Zahra

Rue Jebel Lakhdar

Bab Doukkala Mosque

Hammam

Bab Doukkala

Derb Assehbe

Rue Fatima Zahra

La Maison Arabe

Riad Kniza Musée & Galerie

Rue Boutouil

Bab Doukkala

Rue El Adala

Town Hall

200 m
0.1 miles

Sights

Pikala Bikes

CYCLING

1 ◉ MAP P110, D2

This Dutch-funded nonprofit organisation is a community project on a mission to get young Marrakshis to ditch motorbike aspirations in favour of good, old-fashioned cycling. Group cycling tours depart from its Riad Laârous garage most mornings at 9.30am and include a backstreet tea break and interesting cultural insights. Proceeds pay to train young local men and women as mechanics or professional tour guides. (pikalabikes.com)

Riad Kniza Musée & Galerie

MUSEUM

2 ◉ MAP P110, A2

This private museum has been a labour of love for owner Mohammed, who used to run the respected Al Badii antique shop in Gueliz. When his family closed the shop, the big question was what to do with his overflowing collection of Moroccan antiques. The answer was this lovely little museum, which is split into rural and urban culture, displaying High Atlas carpets, tribal jewellery and clothing, decorative Fez pottery dating to the 17th century and a wonderful collection of Amazigh sugar hammers. (riadkniza.com)

Riad Kniza Musée & Galerie

Musée du Parfum   MUSEUM

3 ◉ MAP P110, F1

This small perfume museum explores Morocco's love affair with essential oils. Rooms cover topics such as hammam rituals, the cosmetic benefits of argan and prickly pear oils, and the role of aromatherapy, herbs and spices in Moroccan culture. If you're into things olfactory, you can even sign up for a workshop to create your own perfume (Dh400 to Dh600). The shady courtyard cafe is a relaxing place for a pot of tea. (benchaabane.com/lemuseeduparfum)

Dar Anis Yoga Studio   YOGA

4 ◉ MAP P110, C4

What could be more convenient than a breezy riad-based studio on the edge of the medina with daily drop-in classes? Owners Philippe and Stephanie have converted their former home into this contemporary, fuss-free yoga space. The tiled courtyard, air-conditioned salon and terracotta roof provide space for flow yoga, sound bath meditations and SoundMoves restorative yoga.

Stephanie is a certified instructor in vinyasa flow yoga, and she works alongside a resident Moroccan teacher who specialises in hatha, plus occasional nomadic teachers. The studio also hosts Arabic calligraphy classes, sporadic cooking courses and the vegan Namaste Cafe (all by reservation only) and runs a popular half-day wellness retreat including one yoga class, a relaxing one-hour

Musée du Parfum

CELIACHEN/SHUTTERSTOCK ©

Understanding Islam ⓘ

Soaring minarets, shimmering mosaics, intricate calligraphy, the muezzin's call to prayer: much of what thrills visitors in Marrakesh today is inspired by a deep faith in Islam. Islam is built on five pillars: *shahada*, the affirmation of faith in Allah and Allah's word entrusted to the Prophet Muhammad; *salat* (prayer), ideally performed five times daily; *zakat* (charity), a moral obligation to give to those in need; *sawn*, the daytime fasting practised during the month of Ramadan; and *hajj*, the pilgrimage to Mecca that is the culmination of lifelong faith for Muslims. Most Muslims in Morocco are Sunni.

One of the biggest disappointments for non-Muslim visitors to Marrakesh who are interested in Islamic history is that they are not allowed to enter mosques and *zawiya* (saint's shrines). This decree dates back to the French protectorate era when French resident-general Hubert Lyautey banned non-Muslims from entering to avoid conflict. Luckily everyone can see the skilled artisan work on the Koutoubia Mosque's minbar (pulpit) that now sits in Badi Palace (p101) and contemplate the artistry of Islamic design within the Ben Youssef Medersa (p82).

massage and a healthy lunch for €85. (marrakechyogastudio.com)

La Maison Arabe COOKING

5 ⊙ MAP P110, B3

Bab Doukkala's legendary Maison Arabe (p114) restaurant also runs this slick cookery school. Longer classes with high-tech demonstration screens can feel a little impersonal, but this school is one of the only places in Marrakesh where tourists with limited time can book into punchy one-hour courses. Participants cook one dish, accompanied by plenty of interaction with the hosting chef, and then eat together after. (lamaisonarabe.com)

Heritage Spa HAMMAM

6 ⊙ MAP P110, C3

Forget any illusions of authentically local hammams: bliss out in this private spa-hammam with a detoxing black-soap scrub or hot herbal massage. It's housed in a traditional riad with comfy nooks for treatments, free-flowing mint tea and good-quality, 100% natural products. (heritagespamarrakech.com)

Hammam Bab Doukkala HAMMAM

7 ⊙ MAP P110, B3

This restored 17th-century hammam in the southeast corner of Bab Doukkala Mosque has heated *tadelakt* (waterproof limestone plaster) floors, a high cedarwood stepped ceiling in the changing area and a cavernous hot room topped by a burgundy cupola. Staff speak little English; this is a real-deal, mellow hammam busy with locals, particularly from 5pm for women.

Chrab wa Chouf Fountain
FOUNTAIN

8 MAP P110, F2

Marrakesh's medina is dotted with public water fountains, but the Chrab wa Chouf ('Drink and Look') fountain still holds on to shreds of former finery with its intricately carved cedar-wood lintel. Unlike many others, the fountain is still used and you'll likely see passing pedestrians stopping for a quick drink as you admire the artistry.

Vegetarian & Vegan Food

It's somewhat ironic that Moroccans actually eat a lot of vegetarian food at home while meat is reserved for special occasions, but tourist menus would have you believe that locals are meat-obsessed carnivores. Still, vegetarian food is easy to find, even in more traditional restaurants, and there are now also a couple of good vegan options. Vegetarian tajines and couscous are standard tourist-menu options, and Moroccan salad starters can make a meal in themselves.

Eating

La Maison Arabe
MOROCCAN $$$

Also running the cooking school of the same name, (see 5 Map p110, B3) La Maison Arabe's reputation precedes it: this was the first restaurant set up to cater to foreigners in the medina, in the 1940s. It was a favourite of Winston Churchill, and once you experience the service, you'll see why. A long list of local wines accompanies the menu of international dishes and refined Moroccan classics. Complete your feast with *amlou* (argan-nut butter) tiramisu. (lamaisonarabe. com;)

Henna Cafe
MOROCCAN $

9 MAP P110, C3

Herbal teas, detox juices, henna tattoos, book exchange, Darija classes, good conversation... they're all on the menu at this intimate upstairs cafe, where a local *nquasha* (henna artist) draws intricate designs on hands and feet, and you can munch on falafel, salads and *kefta* (meatballs) on the covered rooftop. All profits go to local residents in need. (henna cafemarrakech.com;)

I Limoni
ITALIAN $$

10 MAP P110, F1

I Limoni's lemon-tree-shaded courtyard could be a Parisian patio with its cane chairs and light jazz, were it not for the Moorish tiling

Designer Tips 👍

Kitan (p75) This little workshop and showroom is easily my favourite store. Japanese-born Mae Yamazak brings to life a beautiful collection of handmade clothing and accessories. Several pieces in my wardrobe were made in her workshop.

Corinne Bensimon Maison (Map p110, D3; www.instagram.com/corinne_bensimon) I've long been a fan of Corinne's collection of contemporary interior designs – textiles, oversized candlesticks and leather goods. And all thoughtfully presented to create a chic shopping experience.

Kabana (p53) Stylish Kabana is where I head for sunset cocktails, though one drink often turns into a night out. The terrace affords wonderful views of the Koutoubia Mosque.

Grand Café de la Poste (p137) Centrally located in the heart of the new city, this old classic is a favourite for coffee while catching up on emails or with a friend. Sunday brunch is legendary, as is the interior design and the sweeping central staircase of this former post office.

Berber Lodge (berberlodge.net) Pared back and minimalist, surrounded by an olive grove and only 30 minutes from Marrakesh, Berber Lodge is a must for a lingering Sunday lunch. It's an ideal place to recharge before returning to the bustling energy of Marrakesh.

Casa Lalla Tucked away on the shores of Lalla Takerkoust, or the lake as we say locally, Casa Lalla is my go-to on weekends when craving lunch by the water. It makes for a complete change of scenery, despite being just a short distance from Marrakesh, and the car journey is scenic.

Recommended by Willem Smit,
interior designer, hotelier and owner of House of Augustine (houseofaugustine.com) and interiors shop Studio Augustine (p117).

and hand-painted wooden wall features. It's a bit out of the way, but worth seeking out to relax with a glass of wine and excellent pasta dishes such as ricotta ravioli with parmesan, lemon zest and mint. (☏0524383030; ✍)

Dar Moha MOROCCAN $$$

11 ✖ MAP P110, C3

Mohamed 'Moha' Fedal is Morocco's foremost celebrity chef, and his restaurant in a conveniently accessible corner of the medina is the sort of establishment that locals whisper about with reverence. It's a formal affair, but the bright-blue walls, big pool and mature trees make the dining room a memorable setting for his updated local classics. The evening menu is a five-course extravaganza. (darmoha.ma)

Drinking

Regue Jamaa

CAFE

12 🚇 MAP P110, B3

Watch the comings and goings around Bab Doukkala Mosque from under a straw umbrella on the front terrace of this laid-back cafe. There's a long juice list, from peach to strawberry and avocado with almond, plus slap-up breakfasts and a straightforward menu of Moroccan classics, hamburgers and paninis. (📞 0662392390; 📶)

Shopping

Mustapha Blaoui

HOMEWARES

13 🔒 MAP P110, C3

Treasure hunters rejoice: this is a one-stop shop for all things artisanal. Moroccan lanterns drip from the ceilings of this grand emporium that features well-made delights collected by owner Mustapha Blaoui. Concealed behind an inconspicuous wooden door with no sign, the large space offers a relaxed shopping experience amid several chock-a-block rooms holding everything from cushions and carpets to tables and teapots. (📞 0524385240)

Henna tattoos

Henna Tattoos

Natural henna dye, extracted from the dried leaves of the henna tree, is traditionally applied during celebrations, particularly for the Islamic festival of Eid Al Adha and before wedding ceremonies when women gather to adorn the bride-to-be. Fun fact: only married women get henna on their feet (an easy way for men to identify if somebody is single).

Henna tattoo artists hang out on Djemaa El Fna (p38). Be careful, though: some may use 'black henna', which can contain chemicals known to cause skin allergies, rather than natural henna, which is a reddish brown. Henna Cafe (p114) and Marrakech Henna Art Cafe (p52) both have henna artists on hand and guarantee they use natural henna.

Studio Augustine   DESIGN

14 🔒 MAP P110, C3

Step through the studded cedar-wood door into the world of interior designer and hotelier Willem Smit who presents fashion, curated art, midcentury furniture and local artisan treasures at this well-lit shop. He says he wants to offer a 'slow shopping experience' where you can browse for inspiration and no one will hassle you to buy. Look for artisanal crafts, scents, books, linen and vintage *objets*. (houseofaugustine.com)

V.Barkowski   FASHION & ACCESSORIES

15 🔒 MAP P110, C3

Belgian designer Valerie Barkowski is passionate about handcrafted work and artisanal traditions, and this monochrome-toned store complements the simplicity of her designs. Come for high-quality neutral-coloured towels with colour-flash tassels, handcrafted leather tote bags and cotton dressing gowns fashioned after Moroccan *djellabas* (traditional hooded garments). (https://valeriebarkowski.com)

Soufiane Zarib   ARTS & CRAFTS

16 🔒 MAP P110, D2

Soufiane Zarib has gained a reputation for his quality textiles: he buys his own wool and employs his own weavers to produce carpets that are distinctly Moroccan in style, yet made to his own designs. Ring the bell to be admitted into his airy showroom, where shoppers can browse rugs, handpicked ceramics and furniture in peace. Prices range from Dh1000 to €10,000. You'll find a contemporary cafe with shady parasol seating on the rooftop. (soufiane-zarib.com)

Explore ◎

Gueliz & Ville Nouvelle

Gueliz is the yang to the medina's yin. Here you'll find broad European-style boulevards with art deco history, designer shopping and French-influenced cafe, restaurant and bar culture. It is the traffic-clogged heart of the Ville Nouvelle, the area to the west of the medina walls where the French put down roots in 1912. On its edge is the popular Jardin Majorelle.

The Short List

◦ **Jardin Majorelle (p120)** *Strolling the garden painstakingly revived by a French fashion legend.*

◦ **Musée Yves Saint Laurent (p124)** *Paying homage to YSL's design legacy at his cutting-edge museum.*

◦ **Comptoir des Mines Galerie (p132)** *Getting down with contemporary African art in an art deco office building.*

◦ **Amal Center (p134)** *Savouring Moroccan flavours in the lovely courtyard of this restaurant, which trains disadvantaged women.*

◦ **Barometre Marrakech (p137)** *Sipping Morocco-inspired mixes at this legit Prohibition-inspired cocktail bar that wouldn't look out of place in NYC.*

Getting There & Around

🚕 It costs Dh15 between Djemaa El Fna and central Gueliz.

🚶 It's a 20- to 25-minute stroll from Djemaa El Fna to Gueliz up Ave Mohammed V.

🚌 Bus No 1 goes to Gueliz from the bus stop at the Arset El Bilk garden, near Djemaa El Fna.

Neighbourhood Map on p130

Top Experience 📷
Wander through Jardin Majorelle

French fashion designer Yves Saint Laurent bought Jardin Majorelle in 1980 to save it from property developers. Today it's thronged by around 900,000 visitors a year, making it Morocco's most popular tourist site. It's far from the peaceful oasis it was a decade ago, but it's still an extremely stylish place with magical gardens, art deco architecture and an excellent museum.

◎ MAP P130, E1

jardinmajorelle.com

Bou Saf Saf, Villa Oasis & the Studio

In 1922 Majorelle decided to put down roots in Marrakesh and bought a 16,000-sq-metre palm grove on the edge of the medina, planted with poplars that gave his home its original name, Bou Saf Saf (meaning 'the poplars' in Arabic). The first dwelling built here was Moorish in style, with a traditional adobe tower. It wasn't until 1931, after Majorelle had extended the plot to almost 40,000 sq metres, that he hired French architect Paul Sinoir to design a villa and studio in the art deco style.

The building that has become Instagram-famous (pictured; now housing the Pierre Bergé Museum of Berber Arts) was Majorelle's studio and workshop. The main house, where Majorelle and then Yves Saint Laurent and his partner Pierre Bergé lived, was renamed Villa Oasis by YSL. It remained a private residence until Bergé's death in 2017.

Flora & Fauna

The gardens are home to more than 300 plant species from five continents, mostly collected by Jacques Majorelle over several decades of globetrotting. The gardens were first opened to the public in 1947 but were abandoned after his death until Yves Saint Laurent and Pierre Bergé made it their mission to save them.

Aspiring botanists will be in seventh heaven, but it's a wonderful space to explore whether you're a plant super fan or not. Regular signage includes useful illustrations to help visitors identify everything from Mexican agave to Chinese windmill palms and North African date palms, though it could be more helpful if common names were labelled as well as scientific names.

★ **Top Tips**

∘ Buy your time-sensitive ticket online at least a day in advance. Ideally, book for opening at 8am, especially in summer.

∘ Don't scrimp the extra Dh50 and miss the Pierre Bergé Museum of Berber Arts; it's well worth the cost.

∘ Taxi drivers who wait for customers outside Jardin Majorelle are not obliged to use their meters and will overcharge; walk away and hail a taxi on the main road instead.

✕ **Take a Break**

∘ Inside the gardens, the former servants' quarters house **Café Majorelle**, a lovely, leafy spot for tea or cake.

Pierre Bergé Museum of Berber Arts

Majorelle's electric-blue, art deco studio houses the fabulous **Pierre Bergé Museum of Berber Arts**, which showcases the rich panorama of Morocco's indigenous inhabitants in displays of some 600 artefacts, including wood and metalwork, textiles and a room of **regional traditional costumes** displayed with the flair of a catwalk show. Best of all is the brilliant mirrored chamber displaying a collection of chiselled, filigreed and enamelled **jewels**.

Tourist Damage

Dense thickets of bamboo stretch as high as desert towers, flecked with strong shards of sunlight. Jardin Majorelle's exotic bamboo groves are well known and well loved, but what you might not expect is the immense volume of graffiti. For years, tourists have shown their affection for the site by thoughtlessly etching their initials into the gardens' signature stalks and even into some of the giant succulents.

Not only has this environmental graffiti become an eyesore, but the gardens' botanists have realised that it is damaging the plants. Carving into the plants is now forbidden.

Villa Oasis Gardens

In 2018 the Villa Oasis gardens opened to the public for the first time. Accessed via a pathway draped with bright bougainvillea and distinct from the main gardens, they are arguably the more sumptuous and engrossing of the two and have

Waterlily pond, Jardin Majorelle

Who Was Majorelle?

Although famed for its tenure as the home of Yves Saint Laurent, it was Jacques Majorelle (1886–1962) who gifted the gardens to Marrakesh. He was a French painter from Nancy whose father, Louis Majorelle, was a celebrated art-nouveau furniture designer. It was partly his exposure to the art-nouveau movement – rich with organic motifs – that cemented his lifelong passion for flora and fauna. Majorelle arrived in Morocco in 1917 and was quickly bewitched by the same colours and vibrant street life in Marrakesh that seduced YSL half a century later.

He became known for his Orientalist paintings of North Africa and particularly Morocco – some of the reproduction 1920s travel posters for sale around the medina are his work. The striking cobalt blue of the buildings at Jardin Majorelle are an original feature conceived by Majorelle himself, inspired by the bold Moroccan skies, the shade of blue in traditional Moroccan tiles and the head-turning blue veils of the Tuareg people in the southern Sahara. The colour became known as 'Majorelle Blue' and was even trademarked as such.

greatly enhanced the visitor appeal of the complex.

The residence itself is larger than the studio and more Oriental in design, mixing Marrakesh's signature terracotta red with Majorelle's electric blue and Islamic green on its facade and tiled pyramid roof. The bamboo groves of the main garden give way to giant succulents, cacti and mature palms. There's also a succession of calm-inducing water features filled with koi carp, noisy frogs and lily pads, the largest of which pools around a white-pillared pavilion.

These gardens have significantly increased the space accessible to tourists and are well worth including in your visit.

Yves Saint Laurent Memorial

One of the most popular spots in the garden is the memorial. You'll find it along the back wall on the opposite side of the gardens to the entrance/exit. If you can block out the photographers and Instagrammers, it's a poignant space. The memorial is an ancient Roman pillar, which Yves Saint Laurent and Pierre Bergé found on a beach in Tangier. Bergé, who was both Yves Saint Laurent's business partner and life partner, was added to the memorial after his death in Provence, France, in 2017.

Top Experience 📷
Appreciate Design at Musée Yves Saint Laurent

Yves Saint Laurent's love affair with Marrakesh began in 1966 – by the end of his first visit, he'd acquired the deeds to a house in the medina. The Algerian-born French fashion designer (1936–2008) was fascinated by the artistry and palette of Morocco. In 2017 this museum opened as a homage to his work and the inspiration he drew from his second home.

◎ MAP P130, E1

museeyslmarrakech.com

Daring Architecture

Undoubtedly the most thrilling example of con-temporary architecture in Marrakesh, Musée Yves Saint Laurent rises from a granito base of Moroccan marble and stone, draped in a lace-work of terracotta bricks. The textured arrange-ment of the bricks is designed to resemble the weft and warp of fabric. Step inside and it's a complete contrast, with a silky smooth finish intended to complement the exterior like the lining of a couture jacket.

The museum was designed by Studio KO and was the brainchild of Yves Saint Laurent's partner Pierre Bergé (1930–2017), who wanted to create a repository of the fashion designer's work that was 'profoundly Moroccan'. To this end, the building was designed without external-facing windows, to emulate Mar-rakesh's traditional riads. The terracotta colour of the exterior brickwork mirrors the dominant hue of Morocco's 'Red City'.

Patios

Like a traditional house of the medina, internal patios are an integral design feature of the Musée Yves Saint Laurent. The first is a striking circular walk-through that segues between the museum entrance and internal exhibition spaces. Here a series of stained-glass windows echoes the work of French artist Henri Matisse, who greatly influenced YSL's designs. The second patio forms the heart of the building, a square chamber covered with *zellige* (colourful geometric mosaic tilework) with a giant circular dish that catches the rain. The use of green here is significant, as it's highly prized in both Amazigh and Islamic cultures.

Main Exhibition

The core of the museum is the Yves Saint Laurent Hall, a permanent display of his sketches, rotating haute-couture fashions and

★ **Top Tips**

◦ Jardin Majorelle (p120) is next door to the museum; aim to visit both on the same day.

◦ Combined tickets covering Jardin Majorelle, Pierre Bergé Museum of Berber Arts and Musée YSL must be bought online at least one day in advance.

◦ Tickets for both have an allocated time slot.

◦ Take time to browse the very chic boutiques along Rue Yves Saint Laurent across from the garden.

✕ **Take a Break**

◦ The museum's light-filled **Le Studio** is an upmarket can-teen where stylistas linger over tradi-tional Moroccan and French dishes.

◦ Down the street from the museum, smart **My Kawa** (☎0524310016; 🛜✏️👶) does a roaring trade.

Africa as the Muse

Yves Saint Laurent found career-defining inspiration in the beauty of Morocco, with all its raw forms and pure colours. He marvelled at the gardens of Marrakesh, where nature parades on overdrive, and the brightly hued caftans of women in the medina. He found inspiration in the stark blue skies, the earthen architecture and the dramatic waving dunes of the southern deserts. Nomadic fashions for cuffs and collars are hinted at in his iconic accessory designs.

colour-themed accessories. The backdrop is entirely black – a key colour in YSL's designs – creating a cavernous cocoon pierced only by audiovisuals of the designer's catwalk shows and recordings of him speaking.

On the right-hand wall as you enter, the exhibition starts with a biography of Yves Saint Laurent constructed from personal arte-facts, including a letter sent by YSL to French *Vogue's* editor-in-chief Michel de Brunhoff in June 1954 at the age of 17.

Top-quality temporary exhibitions, which change two or three times a year, are held in a smaller adjacent room.

Pierre Bergé Auditorium

Yves Saint Laurent's attention-grabbing fashion designs owe more than a little to his reverence of the stage and screen. Tapping into this theme, the Musée Yves Saint Laurent incorporates a 150-seat auditorium with state-of-the-art acoustics. It is designed for the projection of films, live perfor-mances and broadcasts of theatri-cal performances from around the world; check the website for the schedule. Outside the auditorium entrance, don't miss the 'Costumi-ère', a fascinating display of the costume sketches YSL made for cinema and the theatre.

Library

By appointment, visitors can ac-cess Musée Yves Saint Laurent's 1st-floor library and study room, an important repository of 5000 books on botany, fashion, and Amazigh and Arab-Andalusian culture. Much of it is the personal collection of Yves Saint Laurent and Pierre Bergé.

Walking Tour 🚶

Gueliz Art & Art Deco Walk

When Morocco became a French protectorate in 1912, the new town of Gueliz was established outside the medina walls. Building over the next three decades was heavily influenced by the art deco movement, and a stroll through this district today reveals ruinous French-era landmarks, revamped deco architecture and a lively art and design scene.

Walk Facts

Start Passage Ghandouri, Rue Yougoslavie

End Rue Imam Malik

Length 1.5km; three to four hours

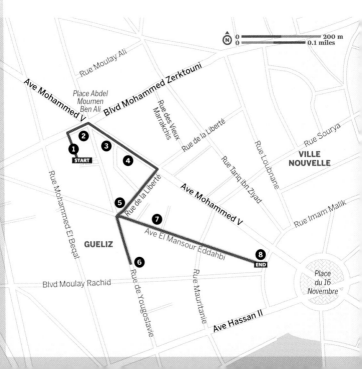

❶ Passage Ghandouri

This mini-shopping centre at 61 Rue Yougoslavie is a haven of art galleries. Begin with **MACMA** (p132) at the end of the passage, an excellent photography gallery with temporary exhibitions. Other galleries in this centre are the **Matisse Art Gallery**, a branch of **Habib Kibari** and showrooms **Yahya Creations** and **Maison ARTC**.

❷ Cafe Culture

Place Abdel Moumen – surrounded by art deco buildings – was once known as the crossroads of cafes because of its cluster of coffee terraces. **Café Atlas** (p138), which dates to the 1940s and has a bold facade mimicking the stern of a ship, is still favoured by coffee-sipping old-timers.

❸ Secret Speakeasy

Nassim Hotel's 1st-floor **Chesterfield Pub** is a fun anomaly. In all appearances, it's a picture-perfect 1930s bar with walnut panelling and stepped cubist design features. Yet the entire hotel was built in the 1990s, designed to blend in to the neighbourhood. Pop in for a beer; it still feels the part.

❹ Through the Camera Lens

Take the once-grand stairway up to **Gallery 127** (galerie127.com), an art deco apartment converted into an industrial-chic art space. Contemporary photography is the medium of choice, and Africa is often the muse.

❺ Journey into African Art

Comptoir des Mines Galerie (p132), the former offices of a mining company, is an impressive reimagining of a once-abandoned art deco building. It is also one of Geliz' best private art galleries, acting as a platform for talent from across the continent.

❻ Crumbling Colonial Epitaphs

Diagonally opposite Comptoir des Mines, check out the ruin of the **Koutoubia Hotel** (once legendary for its nightclub) before strolling down Rue de Yougoslavie to find the abandoned **Ciné-Palace**. This charming art deco cinema opened in 1926, and behind its walls lies a large open-air theatre. It's currently under threat from developers.

❼ Design for Life

Art deco villas are slowly being demolished in Gueliz to make way for bigger new developments, but **Some Slow Concept Store** (p140) is housed inside one that has been saved. Go in to browse contemporary local design.

❽ A Gueliz Institution

It's easy to imagine French office workers and politicians converging on **Grand Café de la Poste** (p137) when it first opened in 1925 as an adjunct to Gueliz' main post office. Now it's an expat favourite.

Gueliz & Ville Nouvelle

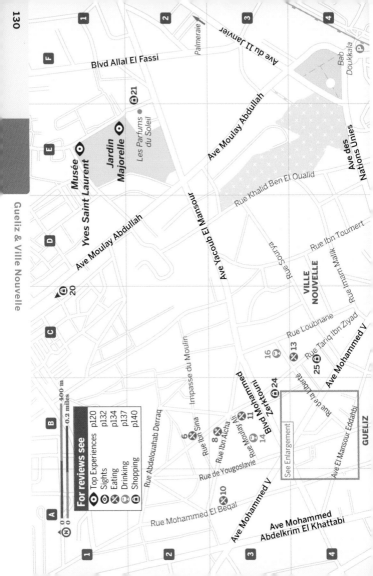

Blvd Allal El Fassi

Palmeraie

Ave du 11 Janvier

Bab Doukkala

Ave des Nations Unies

Ave Moulay Abdullah

Les Parfums du Soleil

◉ 21

Musée ◉ Yves Saint Laurent

Jardin ◉ Majorelle

Rue Khalid Ben El Oualid

Ave Moulay Abdullah

Ave Yacoub El Mansour

Rue Ibn Toumert

Rue Imam Malik

Rue Soukra

VILLE NOUVELLE

▶ 20

Impasse du Moulin

Rue Abdelouahab Derraq

Rue Loubnane

Rue Tariq Ibn Ziyad

16 🍴

13 🍴

25 🍴

Ave Mohammed V

Rue Ibn Sina

6 🍴

8 🍴

Rue Moulay Ali

11 🍴

Blvd Mohammed Zerktouni

14 🍴

24 🍴

Rue de la Liberté

GUELIZ

Rue de Yougoslavie

See Enlargement

Ave El Mansour Eddahbi

10 🍴

Rue Mohammed El Beqal

Ave Mohammed V

Ave Mohammed Abdelkrim El Khattabi

For reviews see	
◉ Top Experiences	p120
◉ Sights	p132
🍴 Eating	p134
Drinking	p137
🛍 Shopping	p140

400 m
0.2 miles

N

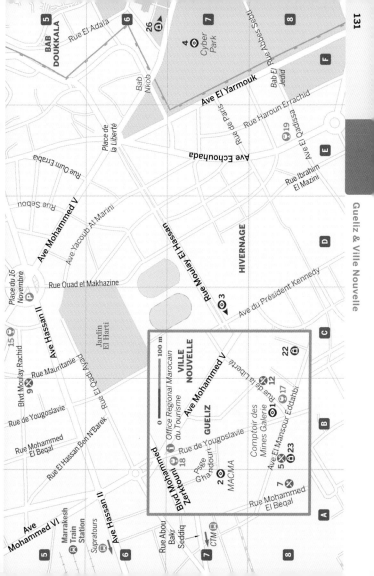

Gueliz & Ville Nouvelle

BAB DOUKKALA

5

6

26

Rue El Adala

Bab Nkob

4
Cyber Park

7

Rue Abbes Sebti

8

Ave El Yarmouk

Bab El Jedid

Rue de Paris

Rue Haroun Errachid

19

Rue El Qadissa

Ave El Qadissa

F

Place de la Liberté

Rue Oum Errabia

Ave Echohada

Rue Ibrahim El Mazini

E

Rue Sebou

Ave Mohammed V

Ave Yacoub Al Marini

Rue Mouley El Hassan

HIVERNAGE

Ave du Président Kennedy

D

Place du 16 Novembre

Rue Ouad el Makhzine

3

15

Ave Hassan II

Ave El Qadi Ayad

Jardin El Harti

100 m

0

VILLE NOUVELLE

Office Regional Marocain du Tourisme

C

Rue Mauritanie

9

Blvd Moulay Rachid

Rue de Yougoslavie

Rue Mohammed El Beqal

Rue El Hassan Ben N'Barek

Ave Mohammed V

GUELIZ

Rue de Yougoslavie

22

Rue de la Liberté

12

17

1

Comptoir des Mines Galerie

Ave El Mansour Eddahbi

5

23

B

Ave Mohammed VI

Marrakesh Train Station

Supratours

Ave Hassan II

Rue Abou Bakr Seddiq

CTM

Blvd Mohammed Zerktouni

18

Psge Ghandouri

2
MACMA

7

Rue Mohammed El Beqal

A

5

6

7

8

Sights

Comptoir des Mines Galerie

GALLERY

1 ◉ MAP P130, B8

Once the home of a mining corporation, this 1932 building now houses Marrakech Art Fair founder Hicham Daoudi's latest project: a contemporary gallery. Restored to its original art deco glory, the sweeping staircases, terrazzo flooring, crystal-shaped wall sconces and furniture make this spot worth a visit in itself. Rotating art exhibitions over three floors profile leading and up-and-coming artists from Morocco and the rest of Africa. (cmgmarrakech.com)

MACMA

GALLERY

2 ◉ MAP P130, A7

In 2019 MACMA's painting archive was moved to its sister venue in the medina, the Orientalist Museum (p87), and this modern gallery shifted its focus to photography, beautifully arranged around a smattering of decorative arts. Images, captured mostly by roving European photographers, span 100 years from 1870 to 1970 and offer an intriguing insight into different facets of Moroccan life, from the chiefs of the High Atlas to urban craftspeople and the women of the northern Rif. Info boards are in English and French. (Musee d'Art et de Culture de Marrakech; ☎0524448326)

Menara Gardens

Marrakesh's Palmeraie

Wrapped up in the legends of Marrakesh's beginnings, this sweep of **palm-studded greenery** northeast of the city is now the haunt of hotels and chichi holiday homes where celebrities take time out from the limelight inside gated complexes. To get any real sense of the pockets of wilderness that still exist, book a trip through the palms by camel, bicycle or on horseback. See our list of tour operators on p20. Many tourists come here for dromedary rides, but be warned that the camels are kept chained to the side of the road.

Top Experiences

Besides palm grove adventures, there are a couple of excellent art museums worth venturing out to the Palmeraie for:

Musée de la Palmeraie (📞 0661095352) Set in a sprawling Andalusian garden of adobe houses, this museum displays an outstanding collection of photography, painting and sculpture. Its 20th-century watercolours, drawings, prints and oil paintings, by Marrakshi artists such as Hicham Benohoud, Abderrahim Iqbi and Larbi Cherkaoui, are particularly strong and demonstrate how local artists have been inspired by Moroccan life and Islamic culture.

Musée Farid Belkahia (fondationfaridbelkahia.com) Farid Belkahia (1934–2014) was one of the most well-known figures in 20th-century Moroccan art. This museum, housed in the artist's old villa, exhibits a selection of his work, including some of the multimedia pieces that he was known for. Refurbishments in 2019 expanded the museum space to display more of Belkahia's works and added a temporary exhibition hall for visiting artists, an auditorium and garden cafe. To get here, follow the signs from Musée de la Palmeraie.

Menara Gardens

GARDENS

3 ◉ MAP P130, C7

Local lore tells of a sultan who seduced guests over dinner and then lovingly chucked them in the Menara's reflecting pools to drown. Nowadays dunking seems the furthest thing from the minds of couples canoodling around the artificial lagoon, or families picnicking amid these royal olive groves. It's arguably Marrakesh's most attractive green space, with its 19th-century pavilion and reflecting pool set against the Atlas Mountains backdrop. Note that climbing the small pavilion is not worth the hefty entrance fee.

The Making of the Ville Nouvelle

When Morocco came under colonial control, *villes nouvelles* (new towns) were built outside the walls of old city medinas, with street grids and modern architecture imposing strict order. Neoclassical facades, mansard roofs and high-rises must have come as quite a shock when they were introduced by the French, but one style that seemed to bridge local Islamic geometry and streamlined European modernism was art deco.

French painter Jacques Majorelle brought a Moroccan colour sensibility to art deco in 1924, adding bursts of blue, green and acid yellow to his villa and Jardin Majorelle (p120). In the 1930s, architects began cleverly grafting Moroccan geometric detail onto whitewashed European edifices, creating a signature Moroccan art deco style that became known as Art Mauresque (Moorish deco). You can still see elements of this style in many of the older buildings in Gueliz. Check out the architecture walk on p128.

Cyber Park
GARDENS

4 ⊙ MAP P130, F7

Stop and smell the roses at this 8-hectare royal garden, dating from the 18th century. It now offers wi-fi (Dh5) at various outdoor hotspots, which draw a steady stream of locals – hence the park's less-than-regal name. At the southern entrance there's a small museum about the history of telecommunications in Morocco, run by Maroc Telecom.

Eating

Sahbi Sahbi
MOROCCAN $$$

5 MAP P130, B8

From the stunning interior by Studio KO to the superb food and friendly service from the all-female team, this restaurant is a winner.

The menu features dishes rarely seen outside a Moroccan home, such as *ftertchetba* soup (worth learning how to pronounce), brains, *brochettes* (kebabs) cooked over the coals or Fez-style chicken *trid* for two. On Fridays its open for couscous lunch, but otherwise only for dinner. (sahbisahbi.com)

Amal Center
MOROCCAN $

6 MAP P130, B2

So many restaurants in Marrakesh reflect poorly on local cuisine, but here you get the real home-cooking deal. And, happily, it's all for a good cause: the Amal Center is a nonprofit association that supports and trains disadvantaged Moroccan women in restaurant skills. Meals are served in a leafy courtyard garden, and the service is warm. (amalnonprofit.org; 📷)

+61

AUSTRALIAN $$

7 MAP P130, A8

The menu is constantly evolving at stylish +61 and aims to capture the laid-back culture of Australia in a thoroughly modern way. Dishes are designed to share, put together with locally sourced ingredients and have a strong focus on seasonal greens. The simplicity of the food is matched by the neutral colour palette of the dining room. (https://plus61.com)

Vita Nova

ITALIAN $$

8 MAP P130, B3

This elegant, Italian-owned restaurant produces consistently good fare: there are good pizzas, a range of antipasti, homemade pasta dishes as well as meat and fish and of course, tiramasù, pannacotta and gelato among the desserts. The conservatory at the front is light and airy. Alcohol is available. There's a separate smoking area. (vita-nova.ma)

Snack Al Bahriya

SEAFOOD $$

9 MAP P130, B5

Fish and chips the Marrakesh way. The intersection of Rue Mauritanie and Blvd Moulay Rachid is packed with sidewalk stalls and restaurants serving up seafood, but simple Snack Al Bahriya is our favourite for dishing up fresh fish and perfectly tender fried calamari with generous (free!) sides of Moroccan bread, olives, lentils and marinated aubergine.

Cantine Mouton Noir

CAFETERIA $$

10 MAP P130, A3

Canadian chef Aniss Meski describes his menu as 'comfort food' from Montreal, and certainly his eggs benedict or the fried banana bread with fruit and maple syrup fit the bill for brunch. There are big slabs of beef, burgers and a focaccia sandwich served in a white-tiled room. A fridge displays

Moroccan Wine

Look for these names on wine menus in Marrakesh restaurants.

White Try food-friendly Medaillon, Le Blanc, Domaine de Jirry or Chateau Roslane Chardonnay.

Gris and Rosé Gris is the term Moroccans use to describe pale rosé wines (like a blush). Domaine de Sahrai is uncomplicated, fresh and always goes down well; look out for Le Gris, Baccari rosé and the crisp, dry top-range Volubilia.

Red Reliable local red wines include the admirable burgundy-style Terre Rouge from Rabati coastal vineyards; well-rounded Volubilia from Morocco's ancient Roman wine-growing region; Ayazi from Chateau Roslane and its spicier merlot-syrah-cabernet sauvignon Coteaux Atlas.

Moroccan
Menu Decoder ⵟⵓ⍓

Let's get one thing straight: Moroccan cuisine is more than tajines and couscous, though you'll find these in abundance. Decode those sometimes rather befuddling Marrakesh menus with the list of popular dishes below.

Amlou Argan-nut butter, spiced with cinnamon and honey.

Bastilla Savoury-sweet pie made of *warqa* (filo-like pastry) layered with pigeon or chicken, cooked with caramelised onions, lemon, eggs and toasted sugared almonds, and then dusted with cinnamon and powdered sugar. The seafood variety comes without the cinnamon and sugar.

Beghrir Pancakes with a spongy crumpet-like texture. Usually served for breakfast.

Bissara Soup of broad beans with cumin, paprika, garlic, olive oil and salt, served for breakfast.

Briouat Cigar-shaped or triangular pastry stuffed with herbs and goat's cheese, meats or egg and then fried or baked.

Harira A hearty soup with a base of tomatoes, onions, saffron and coriander, often with lentils, chickpeas and/or lamb.

Kaab el ghazal Crescent-shaped 'gazelle's horns' pastry stuffed with almond paste and laced with orange-flower water.

Kefta Minced beef laced with ras el hanout spices and parsley, served either as meatballs or as long fingers.

Mahensha Honey-soaked, almond-stuffed coiled pastry.

Sfa Sweet cinnamon couscous with dried fruit and nuts, served with cream.

Sfenj Doughnuts, sometimes with an egg deep-fried in the hole.

Tajine The famous Moroccan stew cooked in a conical earthenware pot. Classic options are chicken with preserved lemon and olives, meatballs in a rich tomato sauce topped with a sizzling egg, and lamb with prunes and almonds served in a saffron-onion sauce.

Tanjia Crock-pot stew of seasoned lamb and preserved lemon, cooked for eight hours in the fire of a hammam.

vacuum-packed meats and jarred goods for sale. There's a kid's menu, too. No reservations. Find it on Instagram @mouton.noir. marrakech. (📞0524434724)

Le Petit Cornichon   FRENCH $$$

11 🍴 MAP P130, B3

Le Petit Cornichon offers exquisite French cuisine in a light and contemporary bistro setting, with a Majorelle-blue streetside patio. Led by the talented Erwann Lance, formerly of the Royal Mansour hotel, the team seek out the finest seasonal produce the medina has on offer to create à la carte and set menus. (lepetitcornichon.ma)

Patisserie Al Jawda   SWEETS $

12 🍴 MAP P130, B8

Care for a pastry, or perhaps 200 different ones? Moroccan patissier Hakima Alami can set you up with sweet and savoury delicacies featuring figs, orange-blossom water, desert honey and other local, seasonal ingredients. Her shop is a lovely, old-fashioned affair where well-heeled Gueliz residents drop by for treats. You pay by weight; just point at what you want. (📞0524433897)

Kilim   MOROCCAN $$

13 🍴 MAP P130, C4

This airy spot is the work of Kamal Laftimi, who launched the popular Nomad restaurant in the medina in 2014. It's his first foray into Gueliz, and he brings a contemporary

take on Moroccan ingredients that's surprisingly lacking here. The menu skips from the likes of watermelon, feta and olive salad to crispy chicken sandwich with harissa mayo and fries. (📞0524446999; 🍴👥)

Drinking

Barometre Marrakech   COCKTAIL BAR

14 🚇 MAP P130, B3

Step into a mad professor's underground lab where apothecary jars and brewery piping line the dimly lit bar. Barometre is a first for Marrakesh: an experimental cocktail bar that wouldn't look out of place in Paris or New York. Eschew the classics for a house special; try the Marrakesh Market with whisky, cinnamon, orange and saffron, or a Moorish Coffee with honey, cinnamon and nutmeg. (facebook.com/barometremarrakech; 📶)

Grand Café de la Poste   CAFE

15 🚇 MAP P130, C5

Restored to its flapper-era glory, this landmark bistro oozes colonial decadence. Prices run high for food, but you can't beat the atmosphere if you want to be transported back to the art deco era when French diplomats built Gueliz. Lap up the old-world ambience of dark wood, fans and potted palms with a coffee, Darjeeling tea or wine in hand. (📞0524433038; 📶)

68 Bar à Vin

WINE BAR

16 MAP P130, C3

A hip and ultralively little wine bar that packs in a nice mixed crowd of Moroccans and foreign residents. There are both European and Moroccan wines on offer as well as beer. Staff are on the ball and friendly. When it gets too smokey later in the evening, escape to the patio bench seating out the front. (0524449742)

MY Kechmara

BAR

17 MAP P130, B8

Want to hang out with the Marrakshi cool kids? Head straight to the covered rooftop bar at Kechmara after sunset and watch it pack out with a buzzing young crowd who lounge on sofas sipping wine and cocktails. Quirky installations, a riot of foliage and flickering candles create a memorable garden-in-the-sky feel. Drinks come with complimentary extras like tapas and spicy juice shots. (https://my-kechmara.business.site;)

Café Atlas

CAFE

18 MAP P130, B7

Café Atlas has anchored Place Abdel Moumen since the 1940s, making it a historic landmark for the Gueliz neighbourhood. A seat beneath the cafe's art deco exterior is a great place to watch the world go by in the company of Marrakshi old-timers. It does decent coffee and breakfasts, and if you sit inside, you can order a beer. (0524448888;)

Barometre Marrakech (p137)

CHRIS GRIFFITHS/LONELY PLANET ©

Moroccan Music

Morocco's indigenous music traditions fall into three main categories, with contemporary musicians often blending both modern and traditional styles.

Djemaa El Fna offers the best opportunity to see travelling musicians each night. If you're in the Kasbah area during the evening, stop by Cafe Clock (p103), which hosts more intimate, local live music acts four nights a week. Saturday nights are dedicated to Amazigh folk music, and a gnaoua band plays on Sundays.

Amazigh Folk

The oldest musical traditions in Morocco are Amazigh (Berber), and there are a variety of different forms that have evolved from the various tribes. The music is usually distinctive for its chanting formula, set to a simple beat.

Gnaoua

Joyously bluesy, with a rhythm you can't refuse, gnaoua began among freed slaves as a ritual of deliverance from slavery and into God's graces. Don't be surprised if the beat sends you into a trance – that's what it's meant to do. A true gnaoua *lila* (spiritual jam session) may last all night, with musicians erupting into leaps of joy as they enter trance-like states of ecstasy.

Arab-Andalusian

Leaving aside the thorny question of where it actually originated (you don't want to be the cause of the next centuries-long Spain–Morocco conflict, do you?), this music combines the flamenco-style strumming and heart-string-plucking drama of Spanish folk music with the finely calibrated stringed-instruments, complex percussion and haunting quarter-tones of classical Arab music.

Modern Moroccan

Like the rest of the Arab world, Moroccans listen to a lot of Egyptian music, but they also have their own home-grown Moroccan pop, rock, hip-hop (called *hibhub*), rap and techno. Although cherry-picking influences from the international scene, many Moroccan bands and singers manage to fuse elements of gnaoua and Amazigh folk into their sound to fashion a musical style that is purely Moroccan.

Comptoir
CLUB

19 🚇 MAP P130, E8

Le Comptoir is one of Marrakesh's most fabled nights out. The glitzy ground floor is reserved for diners and packs out on weekends with Casa playboys, glamour-puss Marrakshis and expat veterans. Up a grand sweeping staircase, the 1st floor morphs into a club space with after-dinner DJs and dancing from midnight. The back garden, strung with star lanterns, is an atmospheric bar. (comptoirdarna.com; 🛜)

Shopping

Sidi Ghanem
DESIGN

20 🏢 MAP P130, C1

Modern Moroccan design fanatics head 4km out of the central city to the industrial district of Sidi Ghanem to scour local designer factory outlets and showrooms. Negotiate a taxi set rate of Dh300 to Dh350 for the round-trip ride from the medina, and score a map of the quarter at an open showroom.

Be aware that opening hours of shops vary, but some close Saturday afternoon and nearly all are closed on Sunday. Bus 15 goes to Sidi Ghanem from Djemaa El Fna.

33 Rue Majorelle
FASHION & ACCESSORIES

21 🏢 MAP P130, F2

More than 60 designers, mostly from Morocco, are represented in this two-floor emporium, and co-owner Yehia Abdelnour dedicates much of his time to sourcing up-and-coming local talent. Quality is high and the prices can be too, but it's still easy to find lovely threads for men, women and children for under Dh1000. Star buys include jewellery, leather handbags, billowing caftans and homewares. (33ruemajorelle.com)

Some Slow Concept Store
HOMEWARES

22 🏢 MAP P130, C8

In a spacious 1936 villa, the Some Slow Concept Store blends the artisanal heritage of Marrakesh with modern-day tastes and trends. Six cosy rooms spread across two floors showcase quality homeware ranges of chic crockery, textiles, lighting and objets d'art. A kitchen pantry selling gourmet artisanal food items leads to a secret vegetarian cafe in a tranquil sunken courtyard. (facebook.com/someslowconcept)

Lalla
FASHION & ACCESSORIES

23 🏢 MAP P130, B8

Find Laetitia Trouillet's stylish hand-crafted bags at her smart boutique in Gueliz. She works with Moroccan artisans to produce these elegant accessories with African, Berber and Middle Eastern accents. Trouillet is French but spends half the year in Marrakesh, and the shop also sells a nicely curated mix of purses, scarves and cheeky t-shirts showcasing local craftsmanship and design. (shoplalla.com)

Move Over, Argan Oil

For decades, argan oil has been Morocco's premier beauty product, but a couple of years ago locals learnt they were sitting on something even more precious: prickly pear oil. Also called the barbary fig, this thorny fruit is sold from carts in Marrakesh's souqs for just a few dirhams between August and October (look out for it – it's a unique seasonal snack). But research has revealed that its seeds have a record content of essential fatty acids, omega 6 and omega 9, and also contain a powerful anti-oxidant that is unique in the plant world.

The unctuous oil from these seeds is now being touted as the next big thing in the anti-ageing market; a wonder drug for scars and dark circles. It's pricey to extract, though – you need at least 15 lorries' worth of fruit to extract just 1 litre of prickly pear oil. Intensive manufacturing methods (it's impossible to do it by machine) mean it's become an extremely expensive commodity, and one you'll see in Marrakesh beauty stores for a minimum of Dh200 for 10ml. Naturom (p56) in the medina and **Les Parfums du Soleil** (Map p130, E2) near Jardin Majorelle are among the stores to stock it in Marrakesh (the former is much, much cheaper!).

Norya Ayron
FASHION & ACCESSORIES

24 🔒 MAP P130, B3

Caftans and *abayas* in flowing silky fabrics and gorgeous prints beloved by top models and actresses from all over the world. While the main branch is in Gueliz, there's a smaller one at Le Jardin Restaurant in the medina. (norya-ayron.shop)

Atelier 44
CONCEPT STORE

25 🔒 MAP P130, C4

Locals from Casablanca and Rabat make the trek to Marrakesh to shop at Atelier 44's collection of fine contemporary Moroccan designers who are keen to showcase their handmade goods in the Red City. The spa downstairs offers a range of treatments, and the owner's background in the cosmetic industry means only the finest products are used (and also line the shelves for sale). (facebook.com/atelier44marrakech)

Ensemble Artisanal
ARTS & CRAFTS

26 🔒 MAP P130, F6

To get a jump-start on the souqs, come to this government-sponsored showcase to see the range of crafts and prices Marrakesh has to offer. Many items are sold directly by producers. The set prices are sometimes higher than in the souqs, but it's hassle-free shopping, and there are toilets, ATMs and a cafe in here so you can take your time.

Survival Guide

Bicycles GARY CHAMBERS/SHUTTERSTOCK ©

Before You Go

Book Your Stay

o Room rates are the highest in Morocco, but Marrakesh has it all: you can sleep anywhere from the funkiest fleapit to palaces straight out of some North African Hollywood fantasy.

o Booking ahead is crucial for medina riads because of the limited number of rooms.

o A city tax (Dh25 to Dh48 per person per night) is payable for each night's stay in Marrakesh. Many properties include this in their quoted rates, but ask guests to pay it separately in local currency upon arrival.

o Note that unmarried heterosexual couples can't get a room together if one person is Muslim.

Useful Websites

Hip Marrakech (hipmarrakech.com) Riad accommodation specialist with a good range of options.

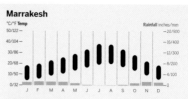

Marrakesh

When to Go

Winter (Dec–Feb) Plenty of blue skies but can be extremely chilly at night.

Spring (Mar–May) Great time for medina escapades with temperatures hovering around 30°C.

Summer (Jun–Aug) Brings scorching heat along with the National Festival of Popular Arts.

Autumn (Sep–Nov) Ideal for non-sweaty souq exploring and sightseeing.

Marrakech Riads (marrakech-riads.com) Professional agency that runs five medina riads.

Marrakech Medina (marrakech-medina. com) Local riad booking agency.

Best Budget

Central House (the centralhousehostels. com/marrakech) Pool, curtained dorm beds, bar, roof terrace – this contemporary hostel in converted riads has it all.

Le Gallia (hotellegallia. com) Great value all around with traditional character and good-

sized rooms around a citrus-tree shaded courtyard.

Equity Point Hostel (equity-point.com) Swags of riad style at backpacker dorm-bed prices. Plus there's a pool.

Best Midrange

Riad UP (riadup.com) This riad wouldn't look out of place in the pages of a design magazine; breakfasts are great.

Riad Helen (riadhelen. com) Light-filled riad with cheery green wooden shutters down a friendly Bab Doukkala alleyway.

Riad Lamdina (riad lamdina.business.site) Comfortable, stylish riad in cool whites with touches of terracotta and green.

Best Top End

Riad L'Orangeraie (riadorangeraie.com) A classy home-from-home with five-star service.

Riad Siwan (riadsiwan. com) Elegant, leafy riad with contemporary touches.

Riad 72 (riad72.com) Italian flair meets Morocco in a plant-filled riad with sensational *zellige* (colourful geometric mosaic tilework).

Arriving in Marrakesh

Marrakech Menara Airport

○ Small, modern **Marrakesh Menara Airport** (marrakesh-airport.com; 📶) is located 6km southwest of town.

○ In the arrivals hall, you'll find currency exchange, ATMs, an information desk and

phone providers where you can equip yourself with a Moroccan SIM card. There's free wi-fi throughout the airport.

○ **Airport bus 19** (Map p46; B5) runs a circular route, every 30 minutes, between the airport and central Marrakesh. It departs across the car park opposite the arrivals hall and stops at Place de Foucauld (a one-minute walk to Djemaa El Fna) and then runs along Ave Mohammed V via Bab Nkob (alight for Bab Doukkala) to Gueliz (passing Place du 16 Novembre and the train station) before heading back to the airport.

○ For a *petit taxi* to central Marrakesh from the airport (6km) the standard set fare is Dh70 by day and Dh105 after 8pm, though drivers will usually ask for more. Taxis waiting at a stand are not obliged to use their meters.

○ If you're staying in a medina riad or out in the Palmeraie, it makes sense to organise a private airport transfer. Riads charge Dh200 or Dh250, and a hotel porter will meet you at the drop-off point and walk you to your hotel door,

so you don't get lost or accosted by local boys.

Marrakesh Train Station

○ Marrakesh's modern **train station** (oncf.ma; 📶) is big, organised and convenient, with ATMs, cafes and fast-food outlets. There's free wi-fi and limited seating. Buy tickets at the staffed counter or from multilingual self-service kiosks. At the latter, you can also pick up tickets pre-booked online. Prices are the same online and at the station, and payment can be made with cash or card.

○ Taxis wait just outside. To Djemaa El Fna, it's no more than Dh15 on the meter (Dh30 at night), but drivers are not obliged to put the meter on if you take one at a taxi rank. You'll also usually be offered a *grand taxi* if you are carrying large luggage, which costs more – around Dh50.

○ City bus 10 (Dh4) heads down Ave Hassan II and Ave Mohammed V to Djemaa El Fna roughly every 20 minutes between 6am and 10pm.

Marrakesh Bus Stations

∘ Marrakesh has three bus stations. **CTM** (ctm.ma) and **Supratour** (supratours.ma) buses arrive and depart Marrakesh from their own stations, situated close to each other in the suburb of Gueliz (walking distance from the train station). There's also the **gare routière** at Bab Doukkala on the eastern edge of the medina. Most tourists use CTM or Supratour buses to reach other parts of the country; there's not much to choose between them in terms of service, price or facilities (both are decent and comfortable).

∘ For CTM and Supratour buses, book in person at the station, an official booking office, or ask your riad to do it for you (their online booking websites are poor). Essaouira is the most popular route; try to book a couple of days ahead.

∘ Taxis wait outside both the CTM and Supratour stations. If you have large luggage you'll have to get a *grand taxi,* which

costs more. Expect to pay Dh20 to Dh50 to Djemaa El Fna.

∘ Bus fares are usually slightly cheaper at the *gare routière,* but the station is swamped with ticket touts and buses often don't leave until they're full (despite what the offices might tell you).

Getting Around

Walking

Compact and flat, Marrakesh was made for walking.

∘ The medina's skinny maze of souqs and alleys can only be explored on foot. These byways are usually shady and would make for pleasant ambling were it not for the speeding motorbikes – walking anywhere in the medina requires vigilance.

∘ Gueliz is laid out like a European city, with pavements for walking, but the lack of shade can make it a hot place to wander around, particularly in summer.

Taxi

∘ Getting a taxi in Marrakesh has improved and most drivers use their meter (ask if they don't put it on).

∘ Avoid taking taxis from stands that get a lot of tourist business (the airport, train station, major hotels, Jardin Majorelle and virtually all those around the medina gates), as they are not obliged to use their meters. You can get a better price by flagging a taxi down from the street.

∘ Note that *petits taxis* take multiple fares at the same time (the meter is programmed to work out who owes what).

∘ If you're trying to hail a taxi from the road, you can theoretically flag down any taxi as long as it has fewer than three passengers already inside. The driver will ask where you're going, and if it's in the same direction as the other passengers, he should let you jump in.

∘ If your party numbers more than three, you must take a *grand taxi,* which are a little harder to find on the roads but not impossible.

Bus

○ The main medina **bus stop** (Map p46; alsa.ma) is on the western side of Arset El Bilk, the garden next to Djemaa El Fna.

○ Services start around 6am and finish between 9.30pm and 10pm, with buses on most routes running every 15 to 20 minutes.

○ Tickets cost Dh4; buy on board using small change.

Key bus lines include the following:

Bus 1 Djemaa El Fna–Gueliz–Bab Doukkala.

Bus 10 Djemaa El Fna–train station.

Bus 11 Bab Doukkala–Djemaa El Fna–Menara Gardens.

Bus 12 Bab Doukkala–Jardin Majorelle–Gueliz–Hivernage.

Bus 15 Djemaa El Fna–Gueliz–Sidi Ghanem.

Bus 16 Djemaa El Fna–Bab Doukkala–Gueliz–northwest suburbs.

Calèche

○ These green horse-drawn carriages congregate alongside Arset El Bilk next to Djemaa El Fna and around Jardin Majorelle.

○ Bargain hard on the cost: a good rate would be around Dh150 for a 1½-hour tour, but many tourists end up paying double that.

○ You can dictate the route to an extent, but a typical tour might run from Jardin Majorelle to the Kasbah and Mellah via Djemaa El Fna, and around the ramparts.

○ Check the condition of the horse before haggling for a ride as some are better cared for than others. Animal welfare charity SPANA (www.spana.org) works with Marrakesh's *calèche* drivers, monitoring horse welfare.

Bicycle

○ This pancake-flat city is good terrain for cyclists, but traffic is a major problem: you'll need to be a confident rider to stomach the medina hubbub.

○ Good quality bicycles and helmets can be hired from **AXS** (argansports.com; ♿) and **Pikala Bikes** (Map p110; D2; pikalabikes.com).

○ Bike-sharing scheme. **Medina Bike** (medinabike.ma) has kiosks at Koutoubia Mosque,

Place de la Liberté in Gueliz and Jardin Majorelle. Register for the service through the app or website.

Car & Motorcycle

Driving in Marrakesh is not for the faint-hearted. Drivers rarely stay in their lane and don't indicate, and you'll have to contend with taxis that stop in awkward places, crowds, *calèches* and donkey carts.

Essential Information

Accessible Travel

○ Narrow medina streets and rutted pavements can make wheelchair access difficult; Gueliz is easier to navigate.

○ Buses in Marrakesh are not wheelchair friendly.

○ *Petits taxis* in Marrakesh can carry a wheelchair on the roof rack, but *grands taxis* are a better bet – they typically cost about 50% more per journey.

○ Only a handful of top-end hotels have

accessibly designed rooms.

o While there are few accessible toilets listed so far, it's worth downloading the Accessaloo app and adding any you find en route.

o Booking ground-floor rooms is essential as few hotels have lifts; accommodation in Gueliz is more likely to.

o Vision- or hearing-impaired travellers are poorly catered for. Hearing loops, Braille signs and talking pedestrian crossings are nonexistent.

o Moroccan guide Houssaine Ichen specialises in accessible travel and comes highly recommended. His website (https://disabled-tourist-guide.com) has good advice.

o For more information, download Lonely Planet's free Accessible Travel guide from https://shop.lonely planet.com/categories/accessible-travel.com.

Business Hours

Marrakesh generally follows the Monday to Friday working week for business purposes.

In the medina souqs many workshops and stalls take Friday (the main prayer day) off, or take an extended lunch break on Friday afternoon.

Banks 8.30am–6.30pm Monday to Friday

Bars 6pm until late

Government offices 8.30am–6.30pm Monday to Friday

Post offices 8.30am–4.30pm Monday to Friday

Restaurants noon–3pm and 7–10pm

Shops 10am–7pm Monday to Saturday

Electricity

Type C
220V/50Hz

Type E
220V/50Hz

Emergencies

Ambulance ☎150

Police ☎190

Tourist Police (Brigade Touristique) ☎0524384601

LGBTIQ+ Travellers

o Marrakesh is Morocco's most popular destination for gay travellers. Foreign same-sex couples usually have no problem when requesting a double bed in hotels and riads, and are unlikely to encounter any problems when out and about, as long as they're discreet.

o Be aware that homosexual acts (including kissing) are illegal in Morocco. If prosecuted and found guilty, jail terms of up to three years and/or a fine can be handed down. Historically, the Marrakesh authorities have turned a blind eye to the laws in regards to gay travellers, but locals can be penalised.

o Don't show affection in public.

o Solo gay travellers should be aware that young male prostitutes operate in the city. Be wary when approached by local men in bars or at Djemaa El Fna.

o Be wary of using social media apps to attempt to access the local gay scene. There have been several cases of foreigners being robbed and physically assaulted after having used the apps to meet up.

o Lesbian travellers are far less likely to encounter any problems.

o Transgender travellers may be subject to abusive behaviour, particularly transgender women. The transgender community does not have a high profile in Marrakesh and education is lacking.

Money

o The medina souqs are still very much a cash society. Only larger shops will accept credit and debit cards.

o Many midrange and top-end accommodation options accept payment in euros.

ATMs

o ATMs are plentiful in both Gueliz and the medina. In the latter, they are usually found along main roads, and there's a cluster around Djemaa El Fna.

o All post offices have an ATM.

o Virtually all ATMs (guichets automatiques) accept Visa, MasterCard, Electron, Cirrus, Maestro and InterBank cards.

o Most ATMs will dispense no more than Dh2000 at a time.

o If you're travelling beyond Marrakesh, note that many of the small villages – including Oukaïmeden and Imlil – have no ATMs. Withdraw money before leaving the city.

Changing Money

o Most banks change cash. Private bureaux de change offer official exchange rates and are open longer hours; however, their rates are typically higher than ATMs.

o Euros, US dollars and British pounds are the most easily exchanged currencies.

Credit Cards

o Major credit cards are usually accepted at top-end accommodation, as well as large tourist-orientated restaurants and shops, though they sometimes incur a surcharge of around 5%.

o Surprisingly, plenty of midrange riads.still don't accept credit cards for room payments.

Tipping

Tipping is an integral part of Moroccan life; almost any service can warrant a tip of a few dirham.

Cafes Leave Dh2.

Museum guides Dh20; more for great service.

Restaurants 10% is standard.

Dos & Don'ts

Photography Do ask before taking a photo of locals.

Alcohol Don't drink alcohol on the street or in public spaces.

Attire Do cover knees and shoulders when in the medina; this applies to men and women.

Ramadan Don't eat, drink or smoke in public during daylight hours.

Language Do try to learn basic greetings. A few words in Darija (Moroccan Arabic) will delight your hosts.

Affection Don't overtly display affection for your partner in public. Hand-holding is fine; kissing is not.

Public Holidays

Banks, post offices and most shops close on the main public holidays, but transport still runs. Religious holidays vary every year depending on the Hegira calendar.

New Year's Day
1 January

Independence Manifesto 11 January

Labour Day 1 May

Feast of the Throne
30 July

Allegiance of Oued Eddahab 14 August

Anniversary of the King's and People's Revolution 20 August

Young People's Day
21 August

Anniversary of the Green March
6 November

Independence Day
18 November

Safe Travel

∘ Marrakesh is, in general, a safe city, but hustlers and touts are part and parcel of the medina experience. Keep your wits about you and be prepared for a fair amount of hassle.

∘ Pillion riders on the motorbikes whizzing through medina streets have been known to grab bags as they pass.

Use a bag you can wear across your body, and walk with the bag next to the wall.

∘ Pickpockets work on Djemaa El Fna and, to a lesser extent, around the medina. Carry only the minimum amount of cash necessary.

∘ Be particularly vigilant if walking around the medina at night.

∘ Hustlers and unofficial guides hang around the medina. They can be persistent and sometimes unpleasant. Maintain your good humour and be polite when declining offers of help.

∘ Check local COVID-related rules before travelling as failure to comply can lead to fines or even a prison sentence.

Telephone Services

∘ To call a Marrakesh landline from inside Morocco, always dial Marrakesh's four-digit area code (📞0524) even when in Marrakesh.

∘ Moroccan landlines begin with 05; mobile numbers start with 06.

Mobile Phones

○ Mobile reception is pretty good in Marrakesh, even in the murky depths of the medina.

○ If you have an unlocked mobile phone, you can buy a Moroccan SIM card at the airport on arrival and at any mobile network provider store.

○ Morocco's GSM mobile phone networks include Maroc Telecom (www.iam.ma), Orange (www.orange.ma) and Inwi (www.inwi.ma).

○ Prepaid packages vary; for Dh100, you can get 200 call minutes plus 10GB data.

Toilets

○ Public toilets are scattered throughout the medina. Most are decently clean and are staffed by attendants who expect Dh1 or Dh2 as a tip. Look for the 'WC' signs. Otherwise, head to a cafe.

○ Public toilets and toilets in cafes and restaurants often have no toilet paper, so keep a supply with you.

○ Don't throw the paper into the toilet as the plumbing is often dodgy; instead discard it in the bin provided.

Tourist Information

Office Regional Marocain du Tourisme (Map p130, B7; ☎ 0524436179) Offers pamphlets but little in the way of actual information.

Visas

Nationals of 68 countries, including those from the UK, EU, US, Canada, Australia and New Zealand, can enter Morocco visa-free for up to 90 days.

Women Travellers

Despite what you might hear, Marrakesh is perfectly safe for female travellers. It's an increasingly popular destination for women-only holidays, and consequently locals are used to seeing females without male companions. However, do bear in mind cultural differences, particularly with regards to clothing. See our guide on Appropriate Medina Attire (p56).

○ Harassment usually comes in the form of persistent verbal badgering – it's rare, though not unheard of, for local men to physically harass women.

○ Younger women are more likely to receive hassle from local men, and the more beautiful you are perceived to be, the more attention you will receive; grey-haired women and mothers command more respect.

○ Sadly, women with unusual body adornments – tattoos, piercings and dreadlocks, for example – may experience hassle for sex or drugs.

○ Prepare to be quizzed on where your husband is; it's a cultural habit and locals don't see it as rude or intrusive.

Language

The official languages in Morocco are Arabic, which is used throughout the country, and Tamazight, the language of the Amazigh (Berber) people. Tamazight is spoken by about a third of the population, and is dominant in the Rif and Atlas Mountains. Most Amazigh also speak Moroccan Arabic, and French is still regularly used in the big cities.

To enhance your trip with a phrasebook, visit lonelyplanet.com.

Moroccan Arabic

Moroccan Arabic (Darija) is a variety of Modern Standard Arabic (MSA), but is so different from it in many respects as to be virtually like another language. This is the everyday spoken language you'll hear when in Morocco. Here, we've represented the Arabic phrases with the Roman alphabet using a simplified pronunciation system.

Basics

Hello.	*es salaam alaykum* (polite)
	wa alaykum salaam (reponse)
Goodbye.	*bessalama/m'a ssalama*
Please.	*'afak/'afik/'afakum* (said to m/f/pl)

Thank you.	*shukran*
You're welcome.	*la shukran 'la wejb*
Excuse me.	*smeh leeya*
Yes./No.	*eeyeh/la*
How are you?	*keef halek?*
Fine, thank you.	*bekheer, lhamdoo llaah*

Eating & Drinking

A table for..., please.
tabla dyal... 'afak

Can I see the menu, please?
nazar na'raf lmaakla lli 'andkum?

What do you recommend?
shnoo tansaani nakul?

I'm a vegetarian.
makanakoolsh llehem

Shopping

I'd like to buy...	*bgheet nshree...*
I'm only looking.	*gheer kanshoof*
How much is it?	*bshhal?*
Can I look at it?	*wakhkha nshoofha?*

Emergencies

Help!	*'teqnee!*
Go away!	*seer fhalek!*
I'm lost.	*tweddert*
Thief!	*sheffar!*
I've been robbed.	*tsreqt*
Call the police!	*'ayyet 'la lbùlees!*
Call a doctor!	*'ayyet 'la shee tbeeb!*

Where's the toilet?	*feen kayn lbeet lma?*
I'm sick.	*ana mreed*
I'm allergic to (penicillin).	*'andee lhsaseeya m'a (lbeenseleen)*

Transport & Directions

I'd like a ... ticket.	*'afak bgheet wahed lwarka l ddar lbayda...*
Where is the ...?	*feen kayn ...?*
airport	*mataar*
bus station	*mhetta dyal ttobeesat*
bus stop	*blasa dyal ttobeesat*
ticket office	*maktab lwerqa*
train station	*lagaar*
What's the fare?	*shhal taman lwarka?*

Please tell me when we get to ...
'afak eela wselna l ... goolhaleeya

Please wait for me.
tsennanee 'afak

Stop here, please.
wqef henna 'afak

Tamazight

There are three main dialects among Tamazight speakers, which in a certain sense also serve as loose lines of ethnic demarcation.

In the north, in the area centred on the Rif, the locals speak a dialect that has been called Riffian. The dialect that predominates in the Middle and High Atlas and the valleys leading into the Sahara goes by various names, including Berber or Tamazight.

More settled tribes of the High Atlas, Anti Atlas, Souss Valley and southwestern oases generally speak Tashelhit or Chleuh, also referred to as Tassousit.

The following phrases are a selection from the Tashelhit dialect, the one visitors are likely to find most useful.

Basics

Hello.	*la bes darik/darim (m/f)*
Goodbye.	*akayaoon arbee*
Please.	*barakalaufik*
Thank you.	*barakalaufik*
Yes.	*yah*
No.	*oho*
Excuse me.	*samhiy*

Practicalities

food	*teeremt*
somewhere to sleep	*kra lblast mahengane*
water	*arman*
Do you have...?	*ees daroon ...?*
How much is it?	*minshk aysker?*
I want to go to...	*addowghs...*
Where is (the)...?	*mani gheela...?*
straight	*neeshan*
to the left	*fozelmad*
to the right	*fofasee*
mountain	*adrar*
river	*aseef*
yesterday	*eedgam*
today	*(zig sbah) rass*
tomorrow	*(ghasad) aska*

Behind the Scenes

Send Us Your Feedback

We love to hear from travellers – your comments help make our books better. We read every word, and we guarantee that your feedback goes straight to the authors. Visit **lonelyplanet.com/contact** to submit your updates and suggestions.

Note: We may edit, reproduce and incorporate your comments in Lonely Planet products such as guidebooks, websites and digital products, so let us know if you don't want your comments reproduced or your name acknowledged. For a copy of our privacy policy visit lonelyplanet.com/legal.

Helen's Thanks

To all the Moroccans who helped me in Marrakesh, from driver Fouad to guide Si Mohamed who revealed the intricacies of Djemaa El Fna by night, as well as all those who told me that the square is 'that way', *shukran bizeff*. I'm enormously grateful to the incomparable Omar Chouiyakh for his assistance. And dining out with city experts Stephen di Renza, Mandy Sinclair and Amanda Harford helped to get under the skin of this exciting city.

Acknowledgements

Cover photographs: (front) Man selling strawberries, Peter Adams/ Getty Images ©; (back) Vegetable tajine (p136), Bartosz Luczak/ Shutterstock ©

Photographs pp32–3 (clockwise from top right): Ana del Castillo/ Shutterstock ©; Robson90/Shutterstock ©; Tupungato/Shutterstock ©

This Book

This 6th edition of Lonely Planet's *Marrakesh* guidebook was researched and written by Helen Ranger. The previous edition was written by Lorna Parkes. This guidebook was produced by the following:

Destination Editor
Zara Sekhavati

Product Editor
Katie Connolly

Cartographer
Julie Sheridan

Book Designers
Hannah Blackie, Fergal Condon, Fabrice Robin

Editor Monique Choy

Cover Researcher
Gwen Cotter

Thanks to Chris Andrews, Andrea Dobbin, Karen Henderson, Federica Mancini, Catherine Newble, Darren O'Connell, Nick Reed, Mandy Sinclair, Bart van Poll.

Index

See also separate subindexes for:

⊗ **Eating** p157
⊖ **Drinking** p158
⊕ **Shopping** p158

🍸 Drinking

🛍 Shopping

Our Writer

Helen Ranger

Although British by birth, Helen has spent most of her life in Africa, living at opposite ends of the continent in Cape Town and Fez, but is now happily ensconced on the banks of the Dordogne River in southwestern France. She has contributed to numerous Lonely Planet guidebooks on African destinations and especially enjoys writing about food. Helen runs a bespoke travel consultancy in Morocco and translates art books from French to English. Follow her @helenranger and @conciergemorocco.

Published by Lonely Planet Global Limited
CRN 554153
6th edition – Nov 2023
ISBN 978 1 83869 156 1
© Lonely Planet 2023   Photographs © as indicated 2023
10 9 8 7 6 5 4 3 2 1
Printed in Malaysia